Dear Loy,

Hope you and Sue
enjoy this. And that
Lilit completes your book
in due time!

Carl

CAROLINA: CRUISING
to an American Dream

CAROLINA ESGUERRA COLBORN

iUniverse books may be ordered through booksellers or by contacting:

iUniverse
1663 Liberty Drive
Bloomington, IN 47403
www.iuniverse.com
1-800-Authors (1-800-288-4677)

Because of the dynamic nature of the Internet, any web addresses or links contained in this book may have changed since publication and may no longer be valid. The views expressed in this work are solely those of the author and do not necessarily reflect the views of the publisher, and the publisher hereby disclaims any responsibility for them.

Any people depicted in stock imagery provided by Thinkstock are models, and such images are being used for illustrative purposes only.
Certain stock imagery © Thinkstock.

ISBN: 978-1-4917-6300-1 (sc)
ISBN: 978-1-4917-6299-8 (e)

Library of Congress Control Number: 2015904982

Print information available on the last page.

iUniverse rev. date: 04/30/2015

Acknowledgments

"Maraming Salamat" to the many people who helped me get this book written and published!

At the top of the list is my husband Bill, who made it possible for me to RV in North America, giving me a wealth of experience about which I could write. He was not only my travel companion but also my go-to editor, spending many hours polishing my business, somewhat technical, second language English. Despite a busy schedule, Bill's nephew Bill Pallucca, who has a double *Summa* in English, gave me invaluable feedback. The same is true for Lilybeth Brazones, sister of a dear friend, who has a *Magna* in Psychology. Thanks, too, to my Filipino editor, Chit Aldave-Tribiana, an English major and former colleague at the Institute of Advanced Computer Technology (I/ACT) for helping me edit the manuscript in several rounds.

Other friends gave good advice, too. Some of them have already published books like Linda Hermann of *Parents to the End*, Roberta Dolan of *Saying It Out Loud* and Linda Kennedy of *Brooke's Miracle* from America. So did Bolet Arevalo of *The Most Practical Immigrating and Job Hunting Survival Guide* from Canada. From the Philippines, it was Raju Mandhyan of *The HeART of Public Speaking* and from Australia Tel Asiado of *Inspired Pen Webs*. Other friends were instrumental in getting me started, egging me on, and helping me complete the book. Silly Willy and Fluffy taught me blogging basics. Liz Kranz, Conchita Derkits, and Suzanne Harper gave feedback. Tony Nievera, who took my author photo, taught me basics of photography. Readers of my blog wrote in tips and Facebook friends enthusiastically participated in polls about the title, the cover, and the photos.

They say that "the only ones who truly know your story are the ones who help you write them." I could not include all their names within the narrative, but I listed them all at the back of the book in an Extended List of Acknowledgments. They visited with us; we visited with them, and we met each other at campgrounds or elsewhere for reunions. They include members of our families, former friends from the Philippines and the United States, and new friends we met on the road. Special thanks also go to Ann Gatmaytan, Jingjing Romero and a core network of friends from the Philippines and around the world, who all helped me bring the book to market.

Writing a book would also have been quite an arduous task without those in the technology field who gave us the proper tools to use. I also salute all the writers who inspired me to begin writing a blog and eventually write this book. Special thanks go to travel memoir writers whose best-sellers I tried to emulate. Even if I did not come close to their level, writing about our cruising in North America became a highly satisfying and intensely internal second journey of my life.

Contents

Introduction

Chasing an American Dream

Don't just dream! Dare!

Manila, Philippines; Texas and Washington, United States
Early beginnings to August 2008

Every day my five-foot tall skinny grandmother, widowed twice, walked several miles to poultry farms to buy a few dozen selected eggs and sell them to stall vendors in the wet market for a small profit. She was able to raise her family of five and even set aside hard-earned pesos. Still, she could send only one child to school. She chose my mother, her youngest and her brightest.

Mom became a teacher. During the Japanese occupation, she even learned Niponggo and helped steer many of her town mates in Rosario, Batangas to safety. The war brought her a husband, too, a handsome Army private stationed there. When WWII ended, Dad took her to the city of Manila. Because she had a deaf brother, she was happy she found work teaching the deaf.

Soon a daughter came, and then another, and yet another...until we were five daughters in all! Dad reveled in his girls' attention, always telling us exciting stories about his fighting alongside Americans. I claimed the warmth of his lap and gave free rein to my imagination about this magical land from where these good soldiers came. My fascination for America was born.

My parents built a small shack with wooden slats for a floor and a patchwork of galvanized iron sheets for a roof on a tiny parcel of land they rented in the city. It was beside a murky and foul-smelling creek. I fell into this polluted body of water once as I reached for the *manzanitas* on a tree that grew right at its edge. A tropical hurricane usually raised the water to waist level, and once we lost our roof to the gusty winds. Most of the time, it was heavenly home.

Tragedy struck when my father was found floating in Manila Bay, hands and legs tied. Like many others in a poor country, his case has not been solved. Mom worked hard, finished her graduate degrees, and became Principal of the government's School for the Deaf and the Blind. She was even sent on a year-long government-sponsored scholarship to the Central Institute for the Deaf in the United States to learn how to teach the deaf to speak.

Her letters came with dried yellow, pink, and purple flowers of spring. Other times they came with dried yellow, orange, and red leaves of fall. If she could, she would undoubtedly have sent snow! That was when my fascination turned into an itch. I knew then that I was destined to be in America. But I had to wait. And I waited a long time.

Mom dreamed and dared; she became my idol. Every day I had to walk two miles to a free public elementary school, but I studied hard and graduated at the top of my class. When the American School in the Philippines conducted nationwide exams in search of ten scholars for junior and senior high school, I was one of those chosen. My itch for America turned into love.

When I graduated as salutatorian, the guidance counselor talked to Mom about having me continue my studies in the United States. Mom said we could not afford the living expenses, even with a scholarship. Hugely disappointed, I accepted a government scholarship at the University of the Philippines instead. It was my first chance to go to America, and I lost it.

When I graduated from college, I was led to US multinationals that invested in my training in the field of computers. As I climbed the corporate ladder, a thought smoldered in my mind. If I earned dollars, my hard work would be paid ten times more! In 1986 when the People Power revolution toppled Marcos, the economy went into a downward spin. I escaped to America.

With the help of their caretaker, my three young children wrote and pleaded that I go home. Besides, my boss at the multinational called and said that my old job was still waiting for me. With the ascendancy of Cory Aquino, the widow of Ninoy Aquino, as the arch-rival of Marcos, Philippine economy returned to normal. Chance number two got frittered away.

My career blossomed, and I put my dream on hold. After all, I was already earning enough to lead a comfortable life. But providing for the home and ensuring my children's future came at a hefty price. It meant working hard, pursuing graduate degrees, and being active in professional organizations—things I deemed necessary to stay on top.

This preoccupation combined with my husband's failed experiments with business spelled doom for our marriage. We separated. A long fifteen years after, my request for annulment was granted. I plunged into my career without looking back. On the personal front, I looked around but all I could find were confirmed bachelors, philandering husbands, and young hopefuls.

As a working single parent to three daughters, I was completely burned out by the time I turned fifty. My thoughts for early retirement grew. I had to get out of the fast lane. Right on cue, the ghost of my American dream reappeared. It was different though, no longer to make a fortune, but to find a new lifestyle, the exact opposite of the one I had been trying to prop up. I wanted time to cook a little, teach a little, travel a little, write a little, and love a little. The Philippines was not the place where that last one could happen. At my age, all the good ones were taken.

After twenty-one years of being single, it took a family crisis to make me take action. In 2002 a sister was diagnosed with Stage 3 breast cancer. She fought it with all her might, choosing to live in the refreshing mountains with everything natural, but the cancer could not be stopped. She had long been estranged from her husband and, just in the previous year, her only child had died from complications of a malignant brain tumor. She spent most of her last months with me and my family. It was painful; I did not want to die like her, all alone.

At the same time that she was fighting cancer, I was up to my ears in things to do. I was completing my doctorate, launching the e-procurement hub of the Philippines, helping pro bono with the automation of Philippine elections, and founding a new IT association. Weighing only 101 pounds after digestive problems borne out of stress, I retreated to North America. My eldest Trisha, with her husband and two children, was in Seattle, Washington, United States working with a major bank. Claudine, my second, with her husband and a son, was in Calgary, Alberta, Canada working in the petroleum human resources policy council. My youngest April, still single then, was in the Philippines with an information technology consulting firm. I reasoned that it was time for me to dream and dare, to be a Mrs. Happy in America!

Finding Mr. Right

My younger sister Julie, who had married an American she met online, put up my profile on a site. I met a Texan—a CPA and naturopath who became my pen and phone pal. When I went to Trisha's home on vacation, he came to see me. He invited me to see him in Temple, Texas. Six months later, we were married. Between the much lower stress levels and his expertise, my digestive health was restored in no time. I learned how to cook, and we started working on a book titled *The Art and Science of Everyday Nourishment.* I was to take care of the art, and he, the science. But I found out he was too retired for my travel bug, and we divorced.

Determined to find Mr. Right, I decided not to squander this last chance and stayed in America. Besides, Claudine and Trisha were each having a baby boy! After four sisters, three daughters, and two granddaughters, I was on Cloud Nine! For four months, I cuddled my very first grandson in Calgary. When the second was born, I moved to Seattle. Soon I was not only babysitting in the day, but also teaching in two colleges and a university in the evenings and weekends. I even volunteered as a small business counselor and marketing lecturer for the Service Corps of Retired Executives (SCORE).

Enter a knight in shining armor, Sir William! He was almost as driven as I was if not more. He had been President and CEO of a national business printing company. After that stint, he bought and operated a printing franchise. He had also been a director of the Document Management Industry Association, a member of the church pastoral council, and even part of the Young Republicans' speakers' bureau. It was too bad his wife of twenty-nine years, the beautiful Judy A died of colon cancer. He married Judy B but, despite efforts, this second marriage ended after eight years.

Even if I was not a Judy C, he was willing to try! Besides, undeniably, I was a competent, charming, compassionate C. All he had to do was to escape the Judy cycle. Clearly, our lives were dovetailing into one dizzying direction. For me, it was another daredevil dive; this time into a late age biracial partnership in a foreign land; for him it was his unsinkable belief in coupledom. After all, America thoroughly believes in the maxim: the third time is a charm!

At first, I did not want to go out with Bill. His profile on Match. com was headlined "Looking For Fun." I thought, "Who would want a man who was just looking for fun?" He was a year older than my cut-off age of sixty-two and three inches taller than my ideal height of 5'7". In his profile photo, he was wearing dark glasses. Was he hiding from someone or something? For six weeks, we wrote to each other about travels and business but I rejected all invitations to meet.

When my sister Julie, a World Public Speaking Champion, was to deliver an inspirational talk at my Toastmasters Club, I wanted THEM to meet. She was running the Philippine Institute for the Deaf, the non-profit school in the Philippines we set up in honor of my mother. I thought his print shop could donate free brochures. Yes, I wanted to take advantage of him, shamelessly!

He could not believe his luck when he walked into the room! I was his absolute dream girl, wearing the shortest black mini skirt. Though I was running the meeting, it was he who took the spotlight, gracefully moving around the room, placing printed programs on every chair, and welcoming each new arrival. He oozed charm. This dashing, distinguished old gentleman with platinum hair looked good in his blue and white Hawaiian shirt. I bet he slept in that day; maybe even had a facial! If only he had blue eyes, I thought. I had to redraw my stupid cut-offs quickly.

That first meeting became a 7:00 pm to 4:00 am saga because, instead of just going out for coffee after the meeting, we all had to rush to Trisha's home. She had been at odds with her eldest Krishna, who had been under my care. They were flying her to the Philippines that night to put her under the care of her other grandma. Julie had an early flight home and asked Bill to take me to the airport to help defuse tension. In a single night, he saw Dr. Carol and Miss Hyde: the executive in control and the lady in tears. He couldn't help himself. He was forever hooked.

Soon we went from pen pals to being activity partners and going to farmers' markets, church, and hiking. One night I was hoodwinked into going to a concert of Michel Legrand at Jazz Alley. Bill said, "Do you realize this is our first date?" I almost fell off my seat! Trying to avoid his eyes, I thought, it was okay! By then he had met the ultimate compatibility test, the Seven Qs: Intelligence, Emotional, Moral, Spiritual, Financial, Political, and Desirability Quotients!

Around that time "The Bucket List" had become a box office hit. Like others, I became glued to the metaphor. We took a thirteen-hour drive from Seattle to San Francisco to visit my youngest sister Cherry who had also married an American. Well, throughout the length of uneventful I-5, Bill did not get to play a single CD or turn on the radio. He could not find my OFF button! He nodded in agreement, interjecting other places. On that day, our long bucket list was born.

Three months later, we were engaged. We found each other by chance through a medium many still frown upon, but millions use, the Internet. Although it is common in the United States, a biracial marriage is laden with opportunities for conflict. Bill is a Caucasian with Scottish/Irish heritage established in the country since the 1600s while I had just recently migrated from Asia. Sources of disagreement, especially at our age, would be threefold: culture, gender, and individual. But I had a dream. And I dared.

PART 1

Getting Started

"What is that feeling when you're driving away from people and they recede on the plain till you see their specks dispersing? It's the too-huge world vaulting us...But we lean forward to the next crazy venture beneath the skies." Jack Kerouac

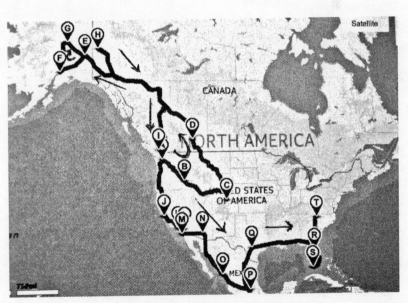

our first cross-continent run

Chapter 1: Choosing to Cruise

Washington, Idaho, and Colorado, United States; Philippines, Taiwan, and Canada
August 2008–August 2009

At first, I wanted the wedding to be on 11/28/08 because by then I would have become a "sexygenarian," and we would have completed six months of engagement. But the Chinese believed 8/8/08 as the luckiest day of the century and fought to open the Beijing Summer Olympics on this day. Numerology won!

Our wedding had to be three things: affordable, fun, and meaningful, a set of values difficult to balance. But then again, so is a marriage. We looked at various options: charming garden estates, well-appointed hotel courtyards, quaint bed and breakfasts, even public parks with earthworks and lots of greeneries. When another couple traded up from the smallest Argosy, we were presented with renting a cruise ship for three hours as the option that made the most sense. Its maximum capacity was sixty-five, taking care of affordability. It was auspicious luck!

August 8, 2008

At 8 pm on 8/8/08, the captain pronounced us man and wife on the upper deck of Champagne Lady on Washington's Lake Union. We had romance, ambiance, food, booze, dance, music, banter, and speeches. We cruised along lovely sights like Seattle's Japanese Garden, the vast University of Washington campus, and the sprawling mansion of a more famous Bill (think Microsoft). But we were most in awe of the haunting copper tanks of a defunct gas company, the romantic *"Sleepless in Seattle"* houseboat and the intriguing sovereign country of Tui Tui!

What could have been more meaningful than a cruise wedding like this for a late-in-life marriage? It was a cruising to a life together of cruising. After all, it was not going to be raising kids, building a home, and saving for retirement. It WAS retirement! We were not going to buy an expensive floating home (as though that was an option). Instead, we were going to visit places that made, or are making, history. We would travel to every nook and corner of the world. It was going to be a life of leisure and payback. After years of hard work to provide for our families, cruising was just what we needed and would still be able to do.

Soon I resigned from teaching and SCORE to focus on just two things: my grandson and my brand new groom. I had already accomplished two of my retirement goals: cook and teach a little. With Bill, I was also sure to love and travel a little. But write? I told myself, if that did not happen, it would be okay. Four out of five would be good enough.

In six short months, Bill sold his printing franchise to a group of local businessmen looking to expand. Then we went on a delayed honeymoon and his first visit to the Philippines where he charmed his way into the hearts of my family and friends. After the Philippines, we went to see his friend in Taiwan who was teaching English as a Second Language. We flirted with the idea of doing the same thing, funding our travels around Asia on weekends, and repeating the formula in other parts of the world. But, after visiting a few centers, we found out that to get working visas, we would have to teach for at least four days a week, leaving us only three days to travel.

We left Taiwan with dreams suspended. On the eighteen-hour flight back to Seattle, we thought, "Why do we need to work to be able to travel? After all, our children have told us to live it up and die broke!" Besides, we do live frugally. Then Bill remembered how he had loved RVing on weekend getaways with Judy A. For Americans, RVing across America IS the American dream.

I had no idea because there are no RVs in the Philippines (the infrastructure just isn't there), only a few celebrity homes on wheels.

I gushed, "Maybe it's time I became a celebrity!" And somebody said, "I would gladly live out of a suitcase if it meant I could see the world!" Well, an RV would be a lot bigger! Besides, traveling around North America first while waiting for my naturalization as a citizen seemed like a better idea than lining up for visas, as we did for Taiwan, for each country we would visit. A US passport will allow entry to 174 countries without a visa or with a visa upon arrival, except for a few countries.

RVing would mean a change of lifestyle. There are three definitions of cruising I considered relevant to this change. The first is to travel about without a particular purpose or destination. Next is to drive at a constant speed that permits maximum operating efficiency for sustained cruising. And the third is to proceed at a moderately fast, easily controllable speed. But I am not including the last definition of cruising reserved for policemen or prostitutes: to wander about slowly, looking for customers or something demanding attention.

I put together my definition. It is an aimless (meaning no humongous aims), effortless (meaning no significant efforts), timeless (meaning no huge dictates on time) drive through life, preferably with a loved one. Being driven means having big goals such as building a home, bringing up kids, or getting an MBA. Cruising, on the other hand, has little ones such as baking a pie, spotting a deer, or taking a photo. Whereas the driven lifestyle needs a lot of energies to sustain, the cruising lifestyle works with whatever energy one may have. Cruisers say: "When I woke up this morning, I had nothing to do; when I went to bed, I was only half done."

Cruising, in a word, sums up the quote: "It is not about the destination. It's the journey." It does not matter where you go, what you do, or who you meet. What matters most is how you proceed from one place to the next. It must be in an aimless, effortless, timeless kind of way—relaxed, not driven; enjoyable, not stressed. And it is better if you have a loved one with you.

No Turning Back

We decided we had better get an RV. There are two general kinds, the motorized ones and those that another vehicle pulls (Please see

Appendix 1 for Different Kinds of RVs). We zeroed in on a motorhome. We decided to look at a Class B or C. They are bigger than a camper van but not as big as a Class A. If we found out we did not really like the lifestyle, we could more easily opt out with a smaller investment. But it still had to have the essentials of "home."

In his classic travel memoir, *Travels with Charley*, John Steinbeck described his camper as something that was "a kind of casual turtle carrying his home on his back." Ours just appeared: a thing of beauty with gentle contour lines, in pale beige and muted brown, freshly detailed. We found her on Craigslist after we lost the Class C the day before as we wavered a little. We were determined not to lose this 1996 Class B 24-foot Telstar by Firan. In an instant, a Star was born!

She was almost like an Airstream but made of lighter fiberglass. She had a little kitchen, a tiny bathroom, an adequate double bed, a cute dinette for four that turned into a guest bed, and a comfortable set of captain's chairs up front. I had always said I wanted a small home. Well, it was the best we could find— 190 square feet! We paid the seller $14,000 in cash and registered Star. That sealed our fate; there was no turning back.

Star on Dempster Highway

We proceeded to rent out our three condos, held three garage sales, posted many treasures on Craigslist, and made $8,000. It was frenzied downsizing! We had to live light for we would be moving our house at ten to twelve miles per gallon. We stored unsold items at Trisha's garage and the storage room of the condo we had lived in, just rented out to a struggling young couple. Next we went to Camping World, a nationwide chain of RV Sales and Services, in Fife, Washington. It had a network of campgrounds (Camping Club USA) that gave discounts on nightly rates and provided a road care assistance program called Good Sam.

Trisha and family were witnesses to what was evolving. April, who had also been bitten by the travel bug, was excited for us even if she was in the Philippines. We decided to show our new lifestyle to our other children in North America: Bill's children, Jim in Boise, Suzanne in Denver, and Cristine in Anchorage, and my Claudine in Calgary.

In June 2009 we took Star to Boise, Idaho, through Snoqualmie Pass and Yakima Valley in Washington, and Pendleton and the Blue Mountains in Oregon. Star gave us such a comfortable ride and a higher and wider visibility from which to take on the sights. Jim, a successful real estate lawyer, his wife, and two kids loved Star. They were more than happy to see that Dad/Grandpa was on to an exciting new adventure!

After Boise, just as we were leaving Provo, Utah, Star sputtered and then stalled along an infrequently traveled canyon. There was no one in sight. Under the sizzling hot sun, I was scared. "Oh no, this may not be a good lifestyle, after all," I cried out. Bill, cool, calm and collected, called Good Sam. In an hour, a tow truck arrived, made a temporary fix and led us back to the Ford dealer in Provo. They replaced Star's fuel pump. Next day we were back on the road!

We spent the night in Moab, Utah, where breathtaking, towering red rocks flanked our campground. The following day we made a quick tour of stunning Arches National Park, catching glimpses of Balanced Rock, Cathedral Rock, Window and other spectacular red sandstone formations. I was thoroughly thrilled and forgot the previous day's scare.

Soon we were in Denver and 24-foot Star just fit on Suzanne's driveway; in Boise, we had parked her along the street in front of Jim's house. Suzanne, who had chosen to be a stay-at-home Mom, her husband, and two kids were delighted with the fascinating nomadic lifestyle of Dad/Grandpa and his new bride. After she had helped us shop for a 32-inch LCD HDTV, a Nikon D5000 SLR, and pots and pans, we were back on the road, on our way to Calgary.

Our GPS showed two well-known tourist spots in Billings, Montana, where we were spending the night. The first was Pompey's Pillar, a five-story rock upon a crevice on which William Clark carved his signature, the only known such writing on the Lewis and Clark route. Then there was the Little Bighorn Battlefield National Monument, marking the spot where American Indians led by Crazy

Horse massacred Lt. Col. George Custer and his 263 men. I was getting excited! American history was unfolding right before my eyes.

When we reached Calgary, Star became a true star, helping Claudine and family transfer to a bigger home. By then, however, we were getting anxious to begin the trek through Alaska Highway on to Cristine. As we drove away from Claudine's new home, I readily drifted into our adventure, leaving behind the familiar, welcoming the unknown. Jack Kerouac had much better words for it: "What is that feeling when you're driving away from people, and they recede on the plain till you see their specks dispersing? It's the too-huge world vaulting us...But we lean forward to the next crazy venture beneath the skies."

Chapter 2: Trekking to Alaska

British Columbia and Yukon, Canada; Alaska, United States
August 2009

The next stop of our adventure was Banff, surrounded by alpine peaks of the Canadian Rockies, often called the Alps of North America. We had visited the town before when we came to see Claudine while Bill and I were still dating. Next to Banff and Lake Louise, the new city of Canmore was also fast becoming another tourist destination, but we were more interested to experience Jasper National Park, deeper into the mountains.

We drove the Icefields Parkway, reputed to be one of the most scenic highways in the world. Majestic purple mountains slowly turned into blazing white peaks. It seemed endless fields of snow draped boundless boulders. At the Columbia Glacial Fields, you can ride huge buses that ply the thick ice. The wheel diameter was taller than my 5'2" frame! I then knew I would see some parts of this world I hadn't even dreamed existed.

At a viewpoint, Bill took a number of photos with our new Nikon DSLR. When he finished taking pictures, I asked to use the camera. He hesitated and appeared irked. Did he think I was criticizing his ability to take photos? Hasn't he seen those Asian tourists with cameras? Doesn't he already know that for us, finding out that you missed a good shot is short of a tragedy? But the beauty before us beckoned, so we swept under the rug what threatened to break out.

Jasper National Park was well worth a visit, even if we were hardly talking with each other. The lakes were elegant in glacial waters of refreshing milky emerald hue. There were many tourists around, but in that Canadian July summer, I felt alone; you could hardly hear a pin drop. But gradually we found each other again in each new scene we saw and in every shot we took. We stumbled upon a useful coping pattern.

The cable car that was supposed to take us up to the top of a mountain for a good view of the entire park was out of order. We changed plans and made a side trip to Mt. Robson instead. It is the highest summit of the Canadian Rockies, almost 13,000 feet tall. At the border of Alberta and British Columbia, we crossed our first Continental Divide (there would be many more). Mount Robson looked as spectacular as Mount Rainier in Washington, even if she rested on a base that was already thousands of feet above sea level. But the two are different. I was analyzing why Mt. Robson's peaks looked more dramatically jagged. "It's not a volcano," Bill said with an impish smile. I scratched my head. I do have to turn off my computer and get closer to nature!

More excitement welled in my heart when we reached Dawson Creek in British Columbia. That was Mile 0 of the intriguing Alaska Highway. The bragging rights were all over town. We had a ball taking photos of ourselves at all the signs. After mass at the local

Catholic Church, we met some of the 300 Filipinos living in the town. I must confess I felt homesick.

We drove slowly on the part of the Highway running through northern British Columbia. There was a lot of wildlife on the roadside. A small herd of bison had been resting when a huge one darted out to our car! A

Mile 0 of Alaska Highway

little scary. Among the grass and wildflowers, a mother bear and her cub played while a moose hid among the shrubs. After Stone Mountain in Liard Springs, we met a Canadian, who said he owned an RV just like Star. He was with his cute wife, another Filipina!

On the Yukon part of the Highway, we encountered the first big town, Watson Lake. Its Northern Lights Museum turned out to be just a brief video of recreated lights on the dome's ceiling for effect, not worth the time and money we and two other couples spent on the show. But the one-of-a-kind Signpost Forest compensated for this fiasco. The Visitor's Centre gave us paint; then we bought a wooden plank from the Home Builder's Centre. Our sign with the words "Bill & Carol, Pittsburg, Ks/ Manila, Phil. 8 pm, 8/8/08" became the 67,000[th] signpost!

On the way to Whitehorse, between Upper Liard and Rancheria, rocky embankments displayed many names assembled from rocks. We thought we could spell out our names, too, but we found out how time-consuming the endeavor was. We just completed the two letters: BC—not British Columbia, not Before Christ, but Bill and Carol. Thus began our practice of leaving some mark of our passing through when the usual warning, "Take nothing but pictures. Kill nothing but time. Leave nothing but footprints," was nowhere to be found.

Before we reached Whitehorse, we stopped at the town called Toad River, composed of a gas station, a restaurant, and a country store—that's it. At a corner of the restaurant, enthusiasts had pinned all kinds of hats. Reluctantly, Bill pinned his prized Taquan Air baseball cap from a fishing expedition with friends in Sitka, Alaska. At this part of the Highway, gas was around $4.50 per gallon, and it was only 2009. But we didn't care. We were having the time of our life!

Whitehorse is the biggest city in the Yukon, so it was appropriate that the world's largest weather vane (in the Guinness Book of Records), a DC3 plane, stood there. Many places had already closed for the season, including the largest fish ladder in the world. We missed seeing salmon jumping out of the river to spawn. Instead, we took a tour of the SS Klondike, one of the biggest boats used for transporting gold on the Yukon River. And then we feasted on a great bowl of chili using the Tim Hortons' gift card given by Claudine. The chain, founded by the famous hockey player Tim Horton, is as ubiquitous in Canada as Starbucks is in America.

Unfortunately, smoke from fifty fires, from Whitehorse to Haines Junction to Beaver Creek up north, stole all our beautiful scenes. We could hardly see anything beyond Star's nose! To understand this phenomenon, we stopped at Burwash Landing, which was previously almost wiped out by a massive forest fire caused by humans camping. We hoped we would never be part of creating such carnage. We found out that lightning is the more common cause, however.

After Destruction Bay, orange flags were everywhere, designating areas damaged by permafrost, a frozen subsurface layer of soil that makes the cost of maintaining the Highway very high. It causes many ripples on the road, creating a roller coaster feel. I thought, at least here nature is the culprit; in the Philippines, it can be corruption! The phenomenon also creates small ponds all along the sides. Evergreens in nearby fields do not grow any taller than a few feet.

Camping in the Kluane RV Park in Haines Junction was a big disappointment. We were supposed to be able to catch a glimpse of Mt. Logan, Canada's highest mountain peak at 19,551 feet, and glaciers in Juneau. We didn't. We also thought we found a great hiking trail near the campground. It was going to be the answer to the absence of fitness centers we loved to frequent in Seattle, our solution to keeping fit while cruising. We didn't. The mosquitoes were big, vicious, and hungry. Because of this (and other reasons) hiking did not take hold as a habit.

At Mile 1422 in Delta Junction, we finally completed our navigation of the Alaska Highway, all the way from Mile 0 in Dawson Creek, British Columbia, in seven days! The signpost at the Visitor Center celebrates this feat, not just of engineering this military supply route, but also of the cooperation between the United States and Canada during World War II.

Reaching Alaska

We reached Tok, Alaska on our first wedding anniversary. At the rate we were going, our anniversaries would most certainly always be at an unforgettable place. It was beginning to feel a lot like a never-ending honeymoon! We got there late in the day, so we had no time to go out for dinner. It was fortunate the campground had a well-patronized café.

The next morning we woke up with the area completely covered with smog from the forest fires that had been raging all around since the day before. Bill called Cristine and told her we would postpone seeing her for a couple of days until the smog dissipated. We headed for Valdez on the southeastern tip of Alaska where it was supposed to be clear.

There were a few showers, the air was damp, and a lot of low-lying fog hovered around. As we lost cell signals and our broadband communications, I commented, "Gosh, the glaciers are puny around here. They are just tiny patches of white." Just a few minutes later, as Star was negotiating a bend in the road, a white hill loomed larger and larger before us.

That hill turned out to be Worthington Glacier, a 113-acre glacier on Richardson Highway, about thirty miles before reaching Valdez, entirely accessible from the roadside. Mr. Adventurer rushed to climb the ice rock. I feigned ankle trouble; I didn't know how dangerous it could be! Soon, he was back with a piece of blue ice which we happily deposited into our freezer.

road accessible Worthington Glacier

In the little fishing town of Valdez, many boats were crammed into its small marina. The longest boat ramp in the world reached far out into the waters that were teeming with spawning pink salmon. We camped at Allison Park near the water. Many budding fishermen lined its banks. On the hiking trails, bears had just ravaged the berry bushes. Up in the hills where the trails wound, we came across a section of the Alaska gas pipeline. But what caught our attention were three young men, wearing flip-flops, hauling a canoe—heavy with provisions and equipment—up the steep trail. They were going camping in the mountains beyond the hills. Cruising is not about age; it's about lifestyle!

At the town thrift store, we chanced upon five Filipinos who worked at Valdez's fish canning factories. They were overseas workers, fighting utter loneliness to send dollars to families they left behind. Such remittances help make the Philippine economy second only to China in Asia. I welcomed the chance to converse in Tagalog again. As usual, I felt somewhat homesick.

When we reached Anchorage, there was no hint of the cold winter that had passed. Cristine thoroughly enjoyed her work and the great Alaskan outdoors. Kyle, her son who was visiting from Hawaii, joined us for a trip to Homer, Alaska (the halibut fishing capital of the world) at the southwestern tip of the state. It has a famous spit jutting out into the cold blue waters of the Bering Sea. The two guys fished to their hearts' content. At night the chef at the motel where we stayed cooked us a fine fish fest from what they caught.

The next day we went hunting for souvenirs and good eats at the shops and restaurants in colorful huts perched above the waters along the spit's shoreline. The largest halibut caught in a derby that day was almost 200 pounds! At the Salty Dawg Café, we had drinks and posted a Philippine 100-peso bill and Cristine's American dollar on its currency-covered ceilings and walls. We will go back someday to each mark we left behind to relive our enjoyment of the place.

Since Kyle had to return to Hawaii, only three of us tried the next adventure: a four-hour Glacier Bay Cruise from Whittier, a small town of about 200 (double during the summer). It is only 62 miles southeast of Anchorage, connected to the road system by a fascinating 2.5-mile tunnel, which alternates as a one-way auto lane and a railroad.

The cruise took us to see twenty-six glaciers up close, some rising to 1,700 feet above sea level. We learned there were three different types: alpine (hanging), piedmont (on mountaintops), and tidewater (on the water edge). Although we did not see any calving (when broken pieces of ice fall into the water and become icebergs), we saw sea otters, seals, porpoises, sea lions, and whales. Then the crew treated us to blue margaritas with ice they had just harvested!

And so from the Philippines to glacial seas, from just a childhood fascination to absolute reality, from a woman alone to a married lady, there I was on the move. My knight in shining armor had me cruising in an RV around the North American continent. Not only will I love and travel a little; but I was also going to do both full-time!' Augustine of Hippo said, "The world is a book and those who do not travel read only one page." Well, Bill and I had just filled our library with a colorful giant book to read for the next few years.

Chapter 3: Becoming as Driven as Before

Alaska, United States; Yukon and British Columbia, Canada
September 2009

It was downright thrilling to be on the go, see new places, and visit family. In just two months, we had traveled through five continental American states, Alaska, and three Canadian provinces. Our pace had been fast; it seemed that we had become as driven if not more than before! It was not the cruising lifestyle we envisioned. But it was exciting, and I didn't mind.

From Anchorage, we proceeded to Denali National Park, established in 1917 as the first national park to conserve wildlife. It was home to North America's highest peak, 20,320-foot Mount McKinley. We briefly passed through Wasilla, hometown of Sarah Palin, to find out if we could see Russia from her balcony (wink!). I was nosy, and Bill was smart, going with his wife's flow. Out of luck, we drove to Talkeetna where the view of Mt. McKinley was supposed to be best. Alas, the mountain was hiding under thick fog cover. We had to get closer.

At the Park, we took a bus to the nearest point to Mt. McKinley, Ieilson. The driver stopped when a black bear suddenly appeared on the road in front of us. Later he showed us Dall sheep grazing on a mountain side, a fox nestled among the grass by the road, and caribous resting down the valley. When we reached Ieilson, the dense fog had not lifted at all. At the gift shop, we couldn't buy any merchandise. They read, "I am part of the 30 percent that saw Mt. McKinley."

We proceeded to Fairbanks and on the University of Alaska campus, we found a viewpoint where we got a glimpse of the High One albeit 100 miles away, with the help of binoculars. At the university's nursery, HUGE artichokes were growing and at the far end of the campus, musk oxen were playing. To see them at a private farm would have cost us Canadian $8 each!

Curious about the Aurora Borealis and the Arctic Circle, we

stopped by the Fairbanks Visitors Center to inquire. We found out there would be a greater probability of seeing the northern lights in five days. In Alaska the way to the Arctic Circle is on Dalton Highway, about 414 miles from Fairbanks to Deadhorse near the Arctic Ocean. In Canada, the way is through Dempster Highway, from Dawson City, Yukon to Inuvik, Northern Territories, about 457 miles. Both were not highly accessible highways to drive on. Bill thought it would be too hard on Star.

We went to North Pole, Alaska instead. Christmas décor hung from all the light posts on the streets. Seven reindeer and a 20-foot Santa marked the campground entrance. A nearby park with real reindeer had its own huge Santa with an authentic sleigh in front. From the big Christmas store on the lot, we sent Christmas cards postmarked North Pole, Alaska dated August 2009 to all our children, grandkids, and siblings. It was a lot of fun being kids again!

Taking a Different Route

We decided to go back to the Lower 48 through a different route, past a town that got its name because the residents couldn't spell "ptarmigan." Chicken, Alaska was a village of thirty-two in summer (seven in winter). Two campgrounds make up the town, one with gold-panning activities, another with a country store. We stayed at the former, up the hill.

Flexibility, I soon learned, was a virtue one must have when RVing. Since we had a new home every four days, taking a bath required brains. Some showers did not have mirrors. Worse, some did not have outlets for blow dryers. The way to mix hot and cold water was different each time. Even the way to pay was always new. I had enough loonies (Canadian coins) for a five-minute hot shower but I ended up having to rinse at the sink. That was not a lot of fun because the room had no heater and, even if it was summer, it was still too cold for me! Bill said I should have inserted a loonie before each time segment ran out, not all at once in the beginning!

The next day, we started our drive through the Top of the World Highway that linked Chicken, Alaska to Dawson City in the Yukon. All we could see were endless mountain tops with alpine tundra in autumnal colors. The United States-Canada border at the Top of the

World Highway was unlike any other; there was not a soul except for Bill, the immigration officer, and me.

To reach Dawson City we all, including Star, had to ride a ferry across the river. The city's "golden" past was kept alive by colorful saloons, thriving general stores, and old theaters in the architecture of the time. We even found the largest gold shovel in the world, a testament to the town's past importance in gold mining. At a street up the hills, almost side by side were the log cabins of two famous authors, Jack London and Robert Service. It was a sign!

Then we made a turnaround. The day we were to go south to Whitehorse, we went north instead, up the Dempster Highway. Yes, we drove to the Arctic Circle! Only about three days and two nights separated us from the bragging rights of reaching the special place. Besides, I had already invested one sleepless night to catch the northern lights. A few other nights in the area would increase my chances. Bill braced himself and Star for the rough journey.

Dempster Highway is what they technically call a dirt and gravel road where rocks are put together, then sealed and packed with mud. Some parts were so rough we had to slow down to five miles per hour. Forty was the fastest Star went; the average was probably twenty-five. At the end of the trip, all her shocks had to be replaced. The mud was so bad that on the way back, it pulled our tailpipe loose. Bill had to crawl under Star and tie it up with his belt. Fortunately, it held until we could get it repaired. Only a heavy-duty washer could remove all the mud that had piled onto Star up to her roof.

Slowly, the trees of the valley changed into shrubs of the subalpine hills; then those turned into moss, lichens, and fungi of the alpine tundra. We had not seen anything like it before. There was some semblance of it at Denali National Park, more at the Top of the World Highway. But here it was in full regalia. We stopped every five minutes to take yet another glorious picture.

By the afternoon a storm had developed, the winds turned nasty, and the cold was biting. We decided to stay at the only campground on the way to the Arctic Circle, Eagles' Nest. Thankfully, we survived the night, tightly keeping each other warm. And the sun was shining again in the morning!

At latitude 66/34 N and longitude 133/36 W, we had reached the Arctic Circle in the Yukon. There was no one and nothing else in sight for miles around. The winds were even more biting. Shivering, we set the timer on the camera, placed it on the lone picnic table, and had the photo of our life taken! Then we hurriedly ran back to the comfort of Star. At that spot, I knew I had found a different phase in my life, with Bill, in America. "Sometimes you find yourself in the middle of nowhere;

the photo of our life

sometimes in the middle of nowhere you find yourself," so goes a saying. Although I still did not see the northern lights, I knew there would be many other chances later.

The next day, going down from the Circle, the colors seemed even more vibrant; more of everything had just turned brighter yellow. We saw an elephant rock on top of a hill, fluted mountains, and little blue lakes. Everything seemed to gather, collect and distil at the Tombstone National Park. That second night we chose to stay at a spot where I thought I saw Dall sheep grazing near the river bank the day before. On the other side of the road was a hill ablaze in fall colors and a Swiss couple who had chosen the spot to camp. We all spent the time looking at the plants up close, to discover how such magnificent tapestry was woven.

Driving Canada's Highways

Right before Watson Lake and the right turn to the Stewart-Cassiar Highway, also known as Glacier Highway, something gave me incomparable joy. The letters BC, which we had earlier formed on the rocky stretch of the Alaska Highway, were still there! I wondered if they would still be there on our tenth wedding anniversary. There will be only one way to find out.

Glacier Highway is a lonely highway through northern British Columbia. For a couple of hours, I was getting bored not seeing a glimpse of a single glacier-topped mountain. In fact, I wondered how the highway got its name, until shortly before the turn to the little town of Stewart toward the coast. Guess what the driven wife asked her dutiful husband to do? Yes, we made the turn!

There was nothing commercial in the town. Just a day off-season, no one wanted to take Bill out fishing on a boat. But we discovered the small town of Hyder (population, 100) at Alaska's southeastern tip, only a mile from downtown Stewart (population, almost 500) at British Columbia's northwestern tip. We will never forget this little town.

From downtown Hyder, we drove up the hill to Salmon Glacier, one of the largest glaciers in North America. Past the old gold mines, she slowly made her appearance beside the 25-mile dirt-gravel mountain road. When we reached the summit, the view was spectacular; I knew of no lens capable of taking that long, wide, stunning view. But, since it was drizzling, Star got another brutal

a third of Salmon Glacier

punishment. It seemed that when you want something badly, you make the impossible possible.

When we came down from the mountain, Salmon Creek had a sideshow waiting for us. For about thirty minutes, a good-sized black bear devoured all the salmon he could find on the water. I had to use my almost obsolete point-and-click camera. Bill could not lend me the Nikon. I certainly did not have the time to sulk. The bear was a mere twenty feet from us, but he didn't seem to notice. By the time he had enough, it was night time, so we had to dry camp nearby. I could not sleep; I was afraid the bear might still be hungry!

On the way out of Stewart, we took the Yellowhead Highway, found a small salmon hatchery in New Hazelton and some of the oldest totem poles in the world in Kitwanga. At a swirling gorge in Moricetown, American Indians, who had the sole rights to fish in the river, were net fishing with their bodies tightly secured by rope. They also owned the camp at the top of the hill. With their pails filled with huge salmon, they allowed us to camp on the river bank instead.

We saw two of British Columbia's contributions to the Guinness Book of World Records: the world's largest fishing rod in Houston and the world's biggest cross-country skis in 100 Mile House on the

Fishing Highway. In Lillooet, nestled among the high foothills of the Rockies, about thirty jade rocks, almost as big as I am, were firmly planted around town. But, on the way out, we paid another price as steep as the grade on those hills. We had to replace Star's brakes.

To catch our breath, Bill booked us at a Vacation Internationale time-share condo at the Clock Tower Hotel in Whistler. With Winter Olympics scheduled for January 2010, preparations were in full swing. We rode the only peak-to-peak gondola in the world, connecting Whistler and Blackcomb mountains, and hiked to the top of Blackcomb for a view of the valley. It was nice to sleep in a king-sized bed, for a change. Although I had come to love cooking in an RV, despite the hassles, cooking with enough counter space was a welcome luxury!

Then the Pacific coast slowly unfolded, leading to Vancouver. We were approaching the city from the north for the first time, and we were surprised by the ginormous boulder that guarded the city. We stopped briefly at Lonsdale Quay for a view of her skyline. As we were leaving Vancouver, we had one lasting thought about Canada: the country is RV-friendly. Every town and Canadian Tire parking lot had a public dump and water station. I love Canada, in summer.

When we crossed the border into Washington, Star's thirst was finally quenched with much cheaper gas. By this time I had been used to surfing the Net for the lowest-priced gas, best-value campground, public dumps, and fresh water stations, and for local attractions we did not want to miss. I had only changed the nature of the project, from business systems to travel adventures! Trisha and family wondered why we were rushing from one place to another, retired but not relaxed. We had surely stumbled upon an anomaly, a driven cruising lifestyle!

Chapter 4: Driving down the West Coast

Oregon, Washington, and California, United States
September–October 2009

Star was not big enough to tow a car. The cost of using her to go from one place to the next, run around nearby sights, little towns, and inside huge campgrounds had been rising. Bill thought a scooter would help and found a slightly used, light blue Yamaha on Craigslist. And just like that, a brand new tandem, Star and Vino, was born. The pair would soon help us roam the land.

We reached Oregon just in time for the reunion of Bill's close high school friends at Sunriver, a private planned resort community of 1,700, without tourists. For a week, we shared an elegant home with eight ensuite bedrooms. The ladies took turns making meals, which became discussions from the liberal left to the conservative right, always with a happy toast to the chefs at the end. Yes, I got mine after serving them chicken *afritada* and fresh *lumpia*!

We biked around the village (Bill and I shared a tandem bike), canoed and picnicked on the banks of the Deschutes River, and dined and shopped in the nearby touristy town of Bend. At the High Desert Museum, we learned about the unique features of the area and hiked the trail at the Big Obsidian Flow, an impressive lava flow of black glass only 1,300 years old. But we were disappointed because smoke from local forest fires hid views of Crater Lake at the National Park. The next day's hike up to Suttle Lake compensated for that and gave us a good view of the Three Sisters, a complex volcano with three peaks, reminding me of my three daughters.

Every day, Bill would steal a few minutes to practice driving Vino because he left Seattle with only a learner's permit. The driver's test had been scheduled in Longview, requiring a day trip back to Washington from the border in Portland. The guys also tried to teach me how to ride a bicycle. But it was all in vain. The conclusion was not only "You can't teach old dogs new tricks," but also "There are people who would never achieve balance, whether in biking or life!"

Then we reached Longview and Bill took his test. Alas, he skidded to the final stop and failed! Worse, he had to wait a week for a retest. We decided to spend the time at Fort Clatsop, Oregon at the southwestern mouth of the Columbia River on the Pacific coast, the end of the westward journey of Lewis and Clark. All along the river, you can still see the original eighty-year-old Douglas fir (about sixty feet in length with twenty feet submerged in the water). These were the log poles used for sorting in the timber industry that developed after the famous expedition.

Leaving Fort Clatsop, we took the Bridge to Nowhere that seemed to disappear into the fog, to Long Beach, Washington. It is the longest beach in the United States at twenty-eight miles and the world's largest drivable beach. It was early October, the air was chilly, and at a distance we saw a huge kite flying. It was a far cry from the color and whizz that fill the skies during Washington's International Kite Festival held every third week of August. Only a mile from the beach is the World

Bridge to Nowhere

Kite Museum, blazing with the colors of its outstanding kite collection. Bill said everyone should know how to fly a kite, so he taught me.

Then it was D-Day; Bill passed! Finally, he could pack me as a charming accessory, a pillion rider while he drove about town. Vino proved handy on our next stops at the Cascade Volcanic Arc. Mounts Baker, Rainier, and Saint Helens in Washington; Mounts Hood, Bachelor, Adams, and the Three Sisters in Oregon; and Mount Lassen in Northern California make up this Arc. They are, just like those in the Philippines, part of the Pacific's Ring of Fire of 160 active volcanoes.

We went back to Crater Lake National Park and this time the views were clear. The lake is almost 600 meters deep, the deepest in the Western Hemisphere and third deepest in the world. Formed 7,700 years ago during the violent collapse of Mount Mazama, it is a nearly symmetrical caldera. Wizard Island, a volcanic cinder cone, dots its middle. The interesting Pinnacles, a group of spires and needles, tower off the land at the southern end of the lake.

Weaving through California

Just past the Oregon-California border, the Cascade Arc's volcanic eruptions created an incredibly rugged landscape with numerous lava tube caves, fumaroles, lava flows, and other volcanic fields. This unique geography is preserved as the Lava Beds National Monument. Twenty-five caves have marked entrances and trails for public exploration. We used Vino to go from one lava bed to another. I felt like a bike dude kind of woman. Trucks passing by might not have meant to, but they covered me with dust! When I saw American Indian petroglyphs, the first I had ever seen, all over Medicine Lake Volcano, I was no longer upset.

Lassen Volcanic National Park is just a hundred miles from the Monument. You can find all four volcano types in the Park: plug (lava dome), shield (tall and broad), cinder (small with a single opening), and strato (composite). The Lassen Peak is the largest plug dome volcano in the world. The rangers warned us of a storm expected later that day, so we had to hurry to avoid getting trapped. Toward the end, plumes of smoke rose from the ground, and, like a young (or old) Yellowstone, the hills were colored with different hues. We lingered awhile to enjoy the scene.

We then found ourselves in captivating Napa Valley, with more than 300 wineries emerging from sunburnt golden fields, a stark contrast to the Cascade Arc's somber arid landscape. We moved from one winery to another, driving Vino, tasting excellent wines, and meeting cheerful people. Bill wanted to stay longer, but we had to be in Mexico by Thanksgiving.

When we got to San Francisco, the City by the Bay, I pigged out on sorely missed Filipino dishes cooked by my sweet sister Cherry who had been teaching little kids to dance at the community center. After this, I had a different kind of nourishment, the latest in Filipino gossip, in Tagalog. Former colleagues from the Institute of Advanced Computer Technology (I/ACT) met us at the trendy Santana Row in San Jose.

Of course, we had to take a side trip to the duo of national parks in central California. Sequoia National Park had a 22-foot limit for RVs but, because it was off-peak, and traffic was nonexistent, they let in Star. To get a good view of San Joaquin Valley, we climbed 300 steps to Moro Rock's observation tower. At the heart of the Park, we found the giant tree, the largest in the world. We were admiring him when we noticed many people milling around another tree, a few meters away. It turned out *that* was the real General Sherman. We couldn't stop laughing!

In Yosemite, Bill had to keep on stepping back far, far into the meadows to take a photo of El Capitan, a HUGE granite rock. Even if it was already October, Yosemite Falls, one of the tallest in the world at 2,425 feet, still looked stunning. Going up Tuolumne Meadows, we found that thin layers of eternal snow still covered mountain tops and meadows. But it was Glacier Point that gave a commanding view of the granite cliffs, notably Sentinel and Half

Bill at Glacier Point, Yosemite

Dome. Bill bravely stood on a cliff for an unforgettably dangerous pose!

We chose to stay at the campground near Yosemite's northern entrance. From there, we were able to roam Yosemite freely with Vino. At camp, we met recent college graduates from North Carolina who had just completed volunteering at the Park before plunging into work. While they fried eggs and grilled hot dogs for dinner, we had a lively chat around the fire. We bonded as an ultimate generation: people who, regardless of age, share cruising as a lifestyle. I decided that my soon-to-be-born blog would be titled: "Generation Z. Cruising in an RV."

Leaving Yosemite, we began our drive down the long California coast from the city of Monterey. We came to Lovers Point, a romantic area of rocks reaching out to the sea with tall cypress trees and stayed for a while. On the 17-mile Drive through million-dollar homes of the rich and famous, we spotted the Lone Cypress, standing on a rock that juts out into the bay. Harbor seals and otters populated enormous rocks in the waters. The whole area is a marine life sanctuary. At Pebble Beach, golfers were braving gusts of wind for the most challenging tee shots of their lives.

Its twin city, Carmel-by-the-Sea, was founded in 1770 in Monterey but, a year later, the Mission San Carlos Borromeo de Carmelo was relocated to its present location. Shops, artists, and a town flourished around it. Even Clint Eastwood is a former mayor. Famous authors including Upton Sinclair, Sinclair Lewis, and John Steinbeck lived there. There go my reminders again!

Those two towns led us to Big Sur, the sparsely populated 90-mile California coastline through which Highway 1 runs and where the Sta. Lucia Mountains rise sharply out of the Pacific Ocean, three miles from the coast. Only about a thousand inhabitants live there, mainly descendants of the original settlers, rich folks from the worlds of entertainment and commerce, and famous artists. Big Sur, Lucia, and Gorda, called "towns," are small clusters of gas stations, restaurants, and motels. There were tourist accommodations, but they were limited and very expensive.

Without any reservation, we found a site at Kirk Creek Campground of the National Forest Service for only $10 a night, after our 50 percent senior pass discount. The trail on the ridge led to a small secluded beach, unsuitable for swimming due to frigid temperatures and unpredictable currents. Back at camp, Bill gave away half of the water in our fresh water tank to thirsty teenagers who had exhausted their supply. That is the kind man that I married! Later, I met a fellow camper who had published two books on Colorado hiking trails. He urged me to write.

Soon we were driving south, and I found out that Highway 1 was right on the edge with thousand-foot drops to the ocean. Star was much taller than a car, and I was at the passenger side from where I could see how we could wind up in a deadly plunge. I nervously held onto my seat. Every five minutes I cried, "Slow down." Bill was driving at an unbelievably fast ten mph!

In the town of San Simeon, I found my reward! Located just south of the 105-foot, 10½-inch Piedras Blancas Lighthouse was the largest elephant seals rookery on the West Coast. As far as our eyes could see, hundreds of those marvelous marine mammals lie on the beach (I was told this scene was repeated many times all the way to Mexico). The males reach up to 16 feet in length and up to 6,000 pounds in weight, conserve body moisture, and just grunt loudly to find mates. Hunted almost to the brink of extinction in the 1800s, they flourished on those beaches.

Once this euphoria subsided, we drove farther along the coast and reached Santa Barbara, the American Riviera. Our first campground was tucked way into the wilderness areas of Los Padres. We went into town using Star because I found riding Vino uncomfortable for longer than fifteen minutes. That meant double parking fees. We transferred to a coastal state park to roam the city with Vino: the first Franciscan mission in California in 1716, State Street, and the wharf.

After Santa Barbara, we drove seventeen scenic miles along the famous Malibu Beach. The homes were huge, some dramatically hanging off cliffs, jutting over the water. Malibu Pier is the historic landmark adjacent to Surfrider Beach, known for its three-point break that offers rides of up to 300 yards. Even in that chilly October afternoon, many surfers were there getting the thrill.

Finally, we reached Los Angeles with lovely coral trees lining its streets. We took in the usual sites: Rodeo Drive, Beverly Hills, the Scientology Center, the Kodak Theater and Grauman's Chinese Theater. After Bill had his photo-op with "Marilyn Monroe," we marveled at the Walk of Fame. More than 2,400 stars, tributes to great achievements in the entertainment industry, are embedded at six-foot intervals over 1.7 miles of Hollywood Blvd. and Vine St.

Later, after taking our photo of the familiar Hollywood sign, we got to think that despite everything LA had to offer, it would not make our list of places we could eventually settle. We just couldn't afford it! But we wore big smiles because the drive down the West Coast that got us there was almost as thrilling as the drive to Alaska and the Arctic Circle!

Chapter 5: Moving on to Mexico

California and Arizona, United States; Sonora, Sinaloa, Jalisco, Guanajuato, San Luis Potosi, and Nuevo Leon, Mexico
October–December 2009

From Los Angeles, we began our drive east to Nogales, the border city where we would cross into Mexico. We stopped in Palm Springs where snow birders were already congregating for the winter and checked in at Western Horizon's Desert Pools, named after three hot tubs of hot, hotter, and hottest. We loved those pools and the campground's other facilities.

When we moved to Thousand Trails' (TT) Palm Springs, it was even better! A tall palm tree marked each campsite. On a Saturday potluck dinner and disco night, we met our first friends on the road. They convinced us to buy into this lifestyle even more by joining a network of campgrounds. Since the price of gas was getting out of hand, Bill was interested. I was interested because campgrounds with improved facilities and lots of activities would make longer stays fun. We placed an inquiry into TT, and they urged us to see them at Wilderness Lakes, north of San Diego. We would be heading east after Mexico, so we had best take a look while in the region.

Furthermore, from TT we would be going to Nogales on a more southern route, and we might not be able to go back to two places we wanted to see. A few miles east of Palm Springs

TT Palm Springs Resort

lies Joshua Tree National Park made up of two contrasting deserts, five spectacular oases, and hosts of Joshua trees that look like men holding their hands up in prayer. We dry camped at one of the nine campgrounds and woke up to what seemed to be unending bright beige boulders. Thirty-five miles south of the Park is Salton Sea at 226 feet below sea level. With salinity at 44 parts per 1000, it should be called the Dying Sea since throngs of dead fish lie on its beaches. Because of this, 30 percent of American white pelicans make it a resting stop on the Pacific Flyway, converting the sea into a fantastic place for bird watching and water recreation.

On the way to TT, we stumbled upon Julian, an unincorporated community (population: 1,621) east of San Diego. Although Julian's hilly setting is picturesque, the town's major draw is apples. Julian apple pies and cider have been hugely popular for nearly one hundred years. And we were there at the heart of the Apple Festival! When we got to TT, Bill immediately signed up for a trial. Even if the cruising pace we were shooting for would have to wait until after our vacation in Mexico, we felt it was time to buy. By that time, we knew we would want to slow down a bit.

On the way to the border, we stopped at the town of Coolidge, Arizona to visit the Casa Grande (Spanish for big house) Ruins National Monument. It is what remains of a four-story structure that had survived extreme weather conditions since the thirteenth century. At the Western Horizon's Casa Grande campground, I discovered Texas Hold'em at just $5 entry fee and played every night we were there. I had forgotten how much fun it was to try to use probability theory I learned while getting a degree in mathematics. I would certainly enjoy card games like this at similar campgrounds.

We decided to look into this other network, just to make sure we were investing in the right one. But, at the presentation, I felt the sales agent was only talking to Bill. I wanted to shout and protest: "I may look like one, but I am not a mail-order bride!" The feeling mounted and, no longer able to hold back my tears, I decided, "That's it! TT it is!"

This incident made me realize that, even after five years, I was still quite a maladjusted immigrant in America. Bill was good at trying to help but sometimes he teased me, too. He would often say, "It's not go down from the car, it's—get out of!" And I would retort, "At least we don't say take a dump; we say "make oo-oo;" it's much cuter! I had even noticed there were many things about which I had no clue, jokes I didn't get, or innuendos I couldn't catch. I came to

America at the "young" age of fifty-four. Bill had to introduce Johnny Carson, twinkies, or Elmer Fudd to me. I looked forward to Mexico. I would be on more familiar ground, and my family would be there!

Vacationing in Mexico

Many have warned us of the hardships of RVing in Mexico. What they didn't know was that nothing had stopped us so far. On November 21 we left the comforts of St. David Resort and headed to Nogales. Surprisingly, the process at the port of entry took only two hours. My broken Spanish (many Spanish words had trickled into Tagalog during Spain's 300-year rule) helped.

Three things struck me while we drove through the Mexican state of Sonora on the road to Mazatlan. First, there were many examples of Mexican spirituality. *Chapelitas*, little chapels that could hold up to three people, dotted the fields on the sides of the highways. Religious sayings, images, grottos or crucifixes adorned the hillsides, much more than I had seen back in the Philippines, which is another predominantly Catholic country.

Second, RVing seemed practically dead in Mexico except for the occasional caravan. On the way to Mazatlan, we used three parks: Sonora RV Park in Hermosillo, Los Mochis RV Park in Los Mochis, and Hotel Tres Rios Trailer Park in Culiacan. They all had spaces for about thirty or more RVs; had water, electric, sewer hookups, WIFI connections, and flush toilets (Los Mochis even had hot showers). But they were eerily empty. We were the only game in town.

Third, this could have been because of the onerous toll fees. From Mazatlan to Culiacan we spent about $40 in fees at six toll booths in 600 miles, practically doubling our camping fee of $20 a night. So we took the Mazatlan Libre (free) route instead of the Mazatlan Cuota (toll) route the next day. Libre was slower with only two lanes, had more potholes (yes, even the Cuota had them), but, as expected, was more scenic.

The rest of the family was waiting for us at Torre Mazatlan, our Vacation Internationale time-share condo. In the mornings young boys walking along the beach, shouting *"Camarrones!,"* would wake us up to a day of frolicking in the beach, pool, and hot tub. On a Sunday, the whole family went to hear mass at the Catedral. As we were leaving, we stumbled upon a lively Mexican fiesta going on in front of the church. Locals in colorful *sombreros* and *boleros* were performing on a makeshift stage. Beside it was a giant Christmas tree made out of Coke bottles filled with glistening liquid in all colors. Next to the Catedral was the *Mercado* where locals buy what they need from a *panaderia, carniceria, fruteria y verduleria,* and *pescaderia.* I even found a shoe repair booth that replaced the velcros on my sandals for $3, quoted at $25 in Oakland, California!

We loved our holiday in Mexico for many reasons. First, the people were helpful and friendly. We were filling up at a Pemex gas station (all owned by the government; one price) in Culiacan when two brothers in a car noticed my helpless look. They came to the rescue and led us to our campground, ten minutes away. Earlier, while we were trying to park at Ley, a grocery chain, a driver got out of his car to remove the carts that were in our way. I even felt like a celebrity as people continually waved at us from the roadsides. Of course, I cheerfully waved back!

Second, the Mexican countryside, just like its Canadian and American counterparts, was beautiful and vast. Agriculture seemed vibrant, the soil more reddish, the weeds brighter and the plants greener. The farmers were into many creative practices, such as the use of greenhouses, white plastic coverings, and irrigation canals. We saw a lot of crop dusters flying. These are things I had rarely seen in Philippine fields.

Third the weather is so much like that in the Philippines. When we left St. David, it was 75°F in the day and 35°F at night. At noon, I would be walking in my swimsuit to the pool but by nightfall I would look for my sweater. In Mazatlan days were in the eighties and nights were in the seventies. I could be in the same shorts and strappy top the whole day!

Then there was the shopping and dining. Zona Dorada is the golden zone in downtown Mazatlan. It is like Santana Row in San Jose, State Road in Santa Barbara, Rodeo Drive in LA, or Palm Canyon Drive in Palm Springs—only a lot cheaper! If you want to get vibrant and colorful Mexican craft and exquisite, intricate or bold, one-of-a-kind jewelry, this is the place to go. And all around the Zona were lots of places to eat authentic Mexican food. The family feasted at the Shrimp Factory with *camarrones* served in many delicious ways.

When Trisha and Claudine and their families left, April stayed behind to seek my help with her application to study for a MBA at the University of Washington. We would be cramped in Star for three weeks, but Bill knew better than not to go along. We stopped for a night in Guadalajara in the Mexican state of Jalisco south of Mazatlan en route to the state of Guanajuato.

At Teotihuacan, April and Bill thought I would not be able to climb the 250 steps of the third-largest pyramid in the world, the Pyramid of the Sun, but I did! From the top, the view of surrounding towns with bright Mexican colors was priceless. This community of ruins, including the Pyramid of the Moon, Jaguar Palace, and Avenue of the Dead, had been meticulously restored so visitors can "relive" the oldest civilization in North America.

back of the Pyramid of the Sun

From our campground in Teotihuacan, we rode the public bus to Ciudad de Mexico, one of the most populated cities (eighteen million) in the world. At the center is the Catedral Metropolitana, built in 1573, the oldest and largest cathedral in the Americas with four facades, twenty-five bells in two towers, and twelve chapels. Templo Mayor, the Aztec Ruins lying below Mexico City, is just beside it, towards the back. The Plaza de la Constitucion is in front; to its left is Palacio Nacional, and to its right the shopping district.

But it was at Avenida Central, some blocks away, where we found beautiful ponchos for only $8, exquisite earrings, for $3 and colorful aprons, for $4. Space is limited in 190-square-foot Star, and April was saving for her MBA, so we just bit our lips. We turned our attention to the spicy, delicious, and inexpensive Mexican street food that lined the sidewalks and feasted on a few.

We completed our sightseeing in the city at Chapultepec (meaning, grasshopper) Hill where the only authentic castle in North America stands. Chapultepec Castle is where Emperor Maximilian I and his consort Empress Carlota lived during the Second Mexican Empire. It is now the Museum of History, of the Spanish and post-Spanish periods, of Mexico. The nearby Museo Antropologia features the pre-Spanish period.

There was one experience in Mexico, however, that we would rather forget. We were supposed to ride the Metro train to our bus station back to Teotihuacan. It was so jam-packed that they had to segregate men from women. We would have ended up in separate cars, so we took a taxi instead. That turned out to be a dangerous ride through the traffic-riddled city. Thank God we survived! Later, Bill discovered he had lost his cell phone negotiating the seas of humanity.

Our first stop going back to the United States was in the state of San Luis Potosi. The campground we were supposed to stay in was out of business, so we settled for one of the best RV Park chains in the world, even in Mexico—Walmart. At Saltillo, our RV Park was better—the back parking lot of a hotel.

Our port of entry was in the state of Nuevo Leon through Laredo, Texas. The vehicles going into America were ten lanes wide. In the end, I was upset because the immigration officers took not only all my plants but also almost everything I had in the refrigerator! But the smile quickly returned to my face as I remembered that we had driven from the Arctic Circle to the Tropic of Cancer in only three months! I couldn't wait for more.

Chapter 6: Looking for Warm Weather

Texas, Louisiana, Alabama, and Florida, United States
December 2009–February 2010

When we were back in the United States, it was already too cold. I wanted to reach Florida by Christmas where the weather should be perfect. It would be a paradise, almost like the Philippines. There we could use our new TT membership extensively and start the real cruising pace. I could almost feel Mark Twain's excitement in *Innocents Abroad* where he wrote, "It was to be a picnic on a gigantic scale."

Our first stop in the United States was at TT Medina Lake, just forty-five minutes away from San Antonio, Texas. Going to the bathhouse or the clubhouse was quite a jaunt, one mile each to the left and right. But it was a lovely woodsy setting. The morning after we arrived, there were twenty-five deer milling around our RV, waiting for some food. April excitedly took photos!

deer waiting to be fed

We took a day trip to San Antonio. At the historic nooks and corners of the Alamo, April learned about the story of 300 brave men and the Birth of the Texas Republic. We took the usual boat ride on the charming River Walk, decorated with all the colors of Christmas. Mariachis were serenading tourists where the boats made a turnaround. By nightfall, we settled in an English Pub. April and I demolished a huge sampler plate while Bill feasted on shepherd's pie.

That night Bill was down with fever. In the morning, we hurried to Houston to the home of one of his close high school friends, Jack, who quickly took him to his doctor. My heart sank. It was pneumonia. A suspicious spot discovered in his X-ray led to an MRI. We stayed a couple of nights more for Bill to get all the rest he needed; Jack's wife

Joy was the complete hostess. A week later, we learned that the MRI had found nothing wrong and I heaved a huge sigh of relief.

Brochures had warned that if you have respiratory problems, you should not go to Mexico. We sadly found out the issue with Mexico was not the economy, the swine flu, or the crime rate. It was pollution! And maybe it wasn't that at all. Maybe the driven pace and our ultra-cramped arrangements for three weeks were also to blame. Bill had also been doing all the driving.

In no time we were in New Orleans, the Big Easy. We chose to stay at the French Quarter RV Resort even if it was not part of TT because we wanted to be just walking distance from where all the action was. Camping fees were top dollar ($69 per night) but because we were also Camping Club USA members, we only paid half. A couple we met at the hot tub invited us for drinks at their Class A motorhome. They had a five-foot Christmas tree! April gushed, "Ma, this is what you and Bill should have!"

Hurricane Katrina must have taken a toll on New Orleans because I remember the French Quarter as smelling better. I attended a global SAP conference in the city in 1998 as the Managing Director of its Philippine subsidiary. I did not have much chance to walk around then. This time I did and got a better feel for the beat of the place. We visited the Cathedral, Café du Monde, the French Market, and the Creole Shop. We also sampled Pat O'Brien's famous drink, Hurricane, and had treats such as gumbo and pralines along the cobbled roads. But I was sad to see April leave. With essays done, she would be spending Christmas with Trisha in Seattle.

Our next stop was another TT campground, Styx River Resort in Robertsdale, Alabama. But it was the nearby town of Fair Hope that we loved. There we discovered a Writers' Cottage, a temporary refuge for traveling writers, behind the public library. One day I may need it. Trees along the streets were all decked with Christmas lights. We separated to look for stocking stuffers. When we got back together, we shopped for our Christmas Eve dinner and ended the day at the Mobile Bay waterfront for some raw oysters at the amazingly low price of $3 a dozen.

In the afternoon of December 24, we finally arrived at the Spirit of Suwannee Music Park at Live Oak, Florida. For the first time, I noticed the beauty of live oaks lavishly draped with Spanish moss from every conceivable branch. It rarely kills the tree because it feeds on nutrients in the air, but the reduced amount of light received by the tree's leaves may stunt its growth. I am glad that live oaks give moss living space. This stamp of peaceful coexistence is all over Florida.

But we had to make the dishes for our small Christmas Eve dinner. The cramped kitchen and dining area made the task quite challenging, especially since we wanted to document our first Christmas away from family. Alas, the camera fell, as Bill was trying to slice the roast turkey beside it. We got the picture, but the camera's short lens was doomed! Maybe we needed more space, not just for visitors, but for ourselves!

Otherwise, the dinner was excellent and the gift giving even more memorable. We had established a new tradition. The Filipino in me couldn't believe I could survive a Christmas celebration without family, but I felt I had all I needed back then. I had Bill. The next day, we danced the night away at "A Tribute to the Eagles" Christmas concert at the Music Park.

Going Further South

Unfortunately, the cold seemed to follow us. Florida was having its longest cold spell in history that year. Days were in 50s and 60s (some 40s) instead of 60s and 70s. Some nights went down to as low as 30s! We consoled ourselves that it was still warmer there than in the rest of the country. We became anxious to move further south where it could be warmer.

Our next resort, Orlando TT, became one of our favorite parks (like TT Palm Springs). It had only the usual facilities, but Disney World was only six miles away! We lost no time in visiting Epcot Center, the theme park for Generation Z. It would have been more thrilling had it not been so unusually cold. Even then, we took on all the rides despite the long holiday lines and waited for the final fireworks that enveloped the giant Christmas tree at night.

On New Year's Eve, the campground threw a party. A hundred couples had their souvenir photos taken under an arch that said: "Cruise to the New Year!" It was quite a big party with hats, noisemakers, finger foods, and booze. All night I blinked with the lights on the Mickey Mouse ears I got from Epcot Center. The Past Tense Band rocked the night away, and when the clock struck twelve, a hundred balloons dropped from the ceiling. Then there was a flood of hugs and a torrent of toasts. Celebrating without family was not a problem in the United States!

From Orlando, we continued south to another TT resort, Peace River in Wauchula, Florida. It was another woodsy campground with the Peace River winding around the sections. Warnings about alligators scared me, but I learned that these were as common in Florida as oranges and huge avocados. Unfortunately, it rained and the place became muddy. Fellow campers said seasonal flooding usually claims a flat section of the resort. Even if we were not in that part, I was afraid the alligators would come too close!

But it was still too cold, so we moved further south to the Keys! It would be like being back to familiar tropical isles. We had been there before and just love the place. Overseas Highway, a long narrow road with blue-green water and swaying palm trees on each side, connects the Keys. It is incredibly beautiful, for us ranking as high as Dempster Highway up and Big Sur.

At Big Pine Key, Sunshine Key Resort owned by Encore (a TT affiliate) was simply wow; the whole Key was the resort! It sat on a piece of sandy land that jutted out into the sea. There was water on three sides and the highway on the other. However, since the sea water was cold, everyone was sunbathing around a good-sized pool instead. A country singer played lively music while tropical drinks were being served for free. The resort had a well-equipped exercise room, a good-sized country store, and a busy marina. The only problem was the restrooms. Designed for tropical weather, they had no doors, not ideal for winter that year. It got cold inside, especially when ocean breeze rushed in while one was still wet.

The scooter trip to Key West would have been too long for me, so we took the public bus instead for only $1.50 per senior. I took absolute pleasure at the driver's asking to check my driver's license to ensure that I qualified for the discount. By 7:30 p.m. we were back at the bus stop, and there met a young man who had slept at a shelter the night before. He traveled the world by sleeping at airports and bus/train depots. "It was too cold, and they gave us blankets," he said. Cruising was not about wealth; it was an attitude towards life. I had to start my blog soon!

We saw more of the Keys during this trip: more shops around

Mallory Square, Truman's Little White House, and the key deer that grow to about three-feet-tall or half the size of the typical deer. On our first visit, we had been to the Hemingway House, the Southernmost Point (ninety-four miles to Cuba) and Sloppy Joe's, Hemingway's hangout, where we danced the night away.

Our next booking was at the Flamingo Campground of the Everglades National Park. Somebody told us about devilish mosquitoes that plagued the area, so we decided to cut our visit short from fourteen to only three days. We were surprised to find that the cold weather delayed the mosquito takeover, a clear benefit of the cold winter!

I had never been close to that many animals before; and, to think, they were all on the endangered list. Anhinga Trail was teeming with anhingas—dark-plumaged long-necked birds called snake birds whose long necks appear above water, looking like snakes ready to strike. It was also teeming with alligators; I counted more than thirty! We took "Beauty and the Beast" photos of each other with

a native Florida alligator

an alligator only a foot away. The estuary had crocodiles, manatees, ospreys, etc. I was happy they said Burmese pythons were just falling out of trees because of the cold! But it was sad to see so many dead fish. It was just too cold for them.

As captivating as animal life was, it did not outdo plant life. The dwarf cypress forests were a sight to behold. Gumbo limbo trees glistened with an almost red brilliance. The red bark is medicinal and was even used by Native Americans to make gumbo soups. The Everglades National Park was such a life-giving environment. Even the night skies were teeming with stars!

Thinking surely the cold weather was over, we started heading back north to spend more days at Orlando TT. And indeed everything was back to normal! We met new people, including the oldest RVers we have known on the road: a ninety-year-old harmonica player and his eighty-three-year-old contortionist-wife. Both are former members of the same circus, and they had been RVing for twenty years in the same 24-foot Class C motorhome (the size of Star). But it was the writer of a now published book that made me wish we had a motorhome just like her 32.5 ft. Class A. I must have sounded almost pleading when I turned to Bill and said, "That's what we need. I would be inspired to write in one of those!"

Chapter 7: Getting Better Equipped

Florida and South Carolina, United States
February–April 2009

We had planned on driving slowly up the East Coast in time for the spectacle of fall in the northeast. We needed to be better equipped for this, so we upgraded our TT membership to Elite status. Not only did this give us more eastern US campgrounds but also twenty-one days at a time instead of fourteen and the park-to-park feature eliminating the requirement for one week out of the system between stays.

We proceeded north to TT Three Flags Resort in Wildwood, Florida for our first-ever 21-day stay at one campground. There were Bingo/Ice Cream Socials on Mondays, Potluck Dinners and Karaoke on Wednesdays, Jam Sessions on Thursdays, Dances on Saturdays, and Gospel Concerts on Sundays. Between playing word games and bridge with couples we met and Texas Hold 'Em with four other guys, my nights were full. There was merit to three-week stays. Real cruising pace indeed has a whole new dimension of fun.

And it gave us time to make real friends. We met Joe and Dottie, both in their 80s, from upstate New York, who had a 26-foot fifth wheel. Our short tour of their RV quickly became a three-hour visit because I found out her favorite games were Scrabble and Upwords, just like mine. While Joe and Bill fished or watched football on TV, Dottie and I played, compared recipes, and then played again. I had finally found my match!

They showed us around The Villages, a group of small gated communities of 77,000 (mostly senior) people and 40,000 golf carts that ran around from recreation centers to shopping malls to golf courses. I could see this place for us in the future. They also took us to nearby Marion County Flea Market that had over a thousand booths, where we bought used DVD movies for $1, and a shopping spree meant shelling out all of $20. The next weekend we were at my first-ever Chili Cook-Off. There must have been fifty booths, and we could have all we could taste for $5. I couldn't go beyond twenty; neither could Joe and Dottie. Bill, Mr. Adventurer, could and did!

Buying Our New Home

Back in Orlando TT, this time for three weeks, there happened to be an RV Show around the Clubhouse. We asked about a 27-foot fifth wheel, the size we thought we could afford. The salesman surprised us with a quote of only $10,000 for the rig and truck after the trade-in of Star and Vino. Financed, it would mean just $140 a month. We could not believe how affordable a bigger RV could be. So we looked at two other fifth wheels on the lot.

In eight months we had traveled 15,000 miles, from Seattle to Alaska and the Arctic Circle to Mexico, and then to Florida. And we were slowly inching into the real cruising lifestyle. We already had an upgraded TT membership. All we needed was a bigger home! Lest you think we bought on impulse, we first discussed the economics of the lifestyle.

We did not have much regular income. Bill's social security had just kicked in the previous month. In addition, we had rentals from our properties and inflow from the sale of his business. But he didn't want to draw from his IRA yet. We wondered whether we would be able to sustain the lifestyle, with the galloping cost of gasoline.

We listed our expenses for the three alternatives we were comparing: 1) living in a home, 2) our previous extensive RVing and 3) the full-time, less driven one we were contemplating. (Please see Appendix 2 for the Five Options in RV Cruising and Appendix 3 entitled Economics of the Cruising Lifestyle). From this analysis, we found out that the full-time RVing Option we were contemplating was even cheaper than living in a home, and the extensive traveling we had just completed was the most expensive way to live!

Buying a bigger "home" was not only possible but it was also the right thing to do! We were already staying longer and running around less. We started knocking on RV doors at campgrounds in December in Alabama, asking the owners to give us a quick look-see of their rigs. After our first 21-day stay in Wildwood, Florida, we had a pretty good idea.

Confident, we went to Tampa, home of the biggest RV dealer in the country, Lazy Days. The company sells more than 7,000 rigs in a year. A huge sign on the main building reads, "Lazy Days. If you love RVing, this is home." They believe that the only profitable relationship in the industry is a long-term one, supplying all the RVs one may need in a lifetime. The 500-acre grounds are always busy with hundreds of RVs coming and going. There are 270+ service bays and an inventory of thousands of rigs. On site are branches of Camping World, Cracker Barrel, Quality Inn, and Flying J. Day-long Starbucks coffee, meals at the Café, a campsite at their exclusive resort, and seminars about RVing are usually complimentary. The staff greets everyone they meet with "Welcome to Lazy Days!"

We formulated a decision matrix for evaluating the five best options that Lazy Days showed us, given our budget (please see

Appendix 4, Criteria for Choosing an RV). The 37.5 foot 1997 Newmar Mountain Aire Class A won! Although a fifth wheel had a close overall score, there would be a greater probability that I would drive a car than a pick-up truck. How smart of my dear husband! The items we

our new Class A Motorhome and dinghy

wanted that were not present in the Mountain Aire, a washer/dryer combo and a flat panel HDTV, were bought and installed. Then we swapped the RV radio with Star's, which had iPod connections. We were even lucky to find a 1998 Saturn already equipped for towing. Then Lazy Days threw in a motorhome towing device for free!

People say it is always a foregone conclusion: when one goes to Lazy Days, he will leave with a new RV. What was initially supposed to be a four-day/three-night look-see turned into an eleven-day/ten-night whirlwind shopping spree! Indeed, when we left, Bill was driving a Class A motorhome and towing a Saturn for a dinghy. But it was sad to say goodbye to Star and Vino.

Sometimes we have to relent; we have to provide ourselves what we need to do it all. We finally had what we needed for a cruising lifestyle. After frantic days, we returned to Wildwood to relax in our brand-new home. The next days were lazy, as I lounged around in the luxury of about 350 square feet of bright new home space, almost double Star's, after letting out the slide. Our new home had seven rooms: an office/den, a living room, a kitchen, a dining room, a bathroom suite, a laundry room, and a bedroom. We also had two TVs and two vehicles! Through Facebook, we invited friends and family from around the world to visit us.

Entertaining in Our New Home

For his birthday, Bill had not only the usual party at the clubhouse but also two dinners at our new home. The first was with Joe and Dottie. The second was with a new couple we had just met, Silly Willy and Fluffy, real-life clowns whose mission is to make children laugh at parties. Their humor blog had 50,000 views in just a year and a half. Through their help, my blog was born!

Then a friend from the Philippines responded to our invitation. Dittas, a bubbly personality I met as a client when I was marketing manager of I/ACT and whom I pirated to join my staff, had grown to be a jet-setting executive of her own. She could visit us after a Texas meeting! We were excited to drive our new motorhome to South Carolina and host her.

En route from Orlando, we passed through St. Augustine, Florida, the oldest city in the United States. When we parked, an enormous entrance that said "Fountain of Youth" grabbed my attention. Alas, it was no miracle cure for the wrinkles that were starting to invade my face. It was a park dedicated to Ponce de Leon who discovered this land in 1513 and called it his fountain of youth. At the Castillo de San Marcos National Monument, the oldest fort in America, they were reenacting the discovery of the land with Spanish-costumed soldiers. Then the historic City Gate opened to the famous walking mall, St. George Street, where we delighted in finding the Oldest Schoolhouse in America in the middle of the shops. But we had to continue north.

We reached the TT Oaks at Point South in Low Country USA. It is an area mostly near or below sea

low-country

level extending from the Sand Hills of South Carolina, just east of Columbia, its capital, to its coast and outlying islands. As far as your eyes could see were marshes filled with low grass and swampy water. It was perfect shrimping country.

Savannah, Georgia is not in the state, but it is often included in the region because it is right at the border and shares much of its history, landscape, and culture. We picked up Dittas at the Savannah International Airport, just forty-five minutes away. We took her on a tour of the city built around twenty-four squares designed in 1733 by Oglethorpe, a British settler. Only twenty-two squares remain. The most beautiful is Monterey, with flowers blooming at the bases of magnificent live oaks. Mercer House, the site of the book and enchanting film, *Midnight in the Garden of Good and Evil*, is on a corner. At another square is the park bench where Forrest Gump contemplated life, likening it to a box of chocolates.

On another day, we drove to the nearby town of Beaufort, an old community dating from 1711, with many old sprawling houses. Historic downtown is home to many southeastern eateries and craft shops, a beautiful waterfront, and a long and winding bridge/ highway to a group of small islands, the farthest being privately owned Fripp Island. But all the shrimp shacks had their seafood deep-fried, so we went to Gilligan's Island to peel steamed shrimps like we're used to.

Dittas loves stately modern homes, so Hilton Head Island was her kind of place. The area was transformed around 1765 by Charles Fraser at the age of twenty-seven, from plantations into pioneering gated communities. Sea Pines was the only one open to the public for a $5 access fee. In Harbor Town, a centuries-old live oak tree named Liberty Oak sheltered enormous rocking chairs. On Coligny Beach, hundreds of umbrellas turned the beach wildly colorful while a huge statue of Neptune told time with his long spear reflected on a giant sundial at Shelter Cove.

On the other hand, Charleston had gorgeous southern mansions. They look out to Fort Sumter on the Bay, where the first blast of the Civil War began. With 300 churches, the city is also known as the Holy City. Dittas was kept busiest at the City Market with hundreds of stalls, flea-market style, selling a variety of Low Country crafts inside a long line of concrete tunnel-like structures. That's where she found a parting gift for us: the yellow Welcome Sign that hangs at our "home."

Our campground was a perfect spot from which to tour the area on some days and stay home to relax on other days. And our new motorhome and dinghy formed the perfect tandem with which to do both. Although the campground did not have many amenities, I will always remember it as the place where I finally beat Bill in billiards. It was also where, one lazy afternoon, we had an experience we would rather forget. As we were taking our brisk walk around the three ponds on the property, I tried to take a photo of Bill. I wanted to fit all the fall colors on the trees mirrored perfectly in the waters on the camera's frame. I urged him to step farther and farther back onto the edge. Suddenly, an alligator jumped; it had been camouflaged, resting on the grass! I hated myself for being so foolish. Bill was, as usual, forgiving. I could have easily been a widow, lonely in the new home we had just started to enjoy.

Chapter 8: Finally, Cruising

North Carolina and Virginia, United States
April–June 2009

We had stayed in Florida for three months, but it was only in the last month after we bought our new home when we started to slow down. In South Carolina, we reverted partly into running around while hosting a friend. But in North Carolina, we stayed in only three campgrounds in nine weeks! And we loved it.

The first three weeks were at the TT Forest Lake RV Resort in Advance (pronounced with the accent on the first syllable). We chilled out, shared dinners with fellow RVers, played mini-golf, billiards, and table tennis and took up pickle ball, yoga, and Pilates. Bill took out a state fishing license and alternated between the Yadkin River, just a hundred feet away, and the small stocked lake on the Resort. While he was drowning worms, I got busy with my blog.

On some days, we ventured out of the campground and wandered around consignment shops and flea markets in downtown Lexington (eight miles away) and Mocksville (ten miles away), hunting for treasures. More often, however, to get faster Internet connection, free movies, and books and magazines we would go to the library (Please see Appendix 5 for Resources around a Campground). One afternoon, we enjoyed a Cracker Barrel dinner in Winston-Salem.

After chilling out in Advance for three weeks, we moved to Bass Lake Resort in Salisbury. I was so glad we chose this resort because there I met the first Asian and Filipina I encountered in the RVing world (I would meet only two!). She introduced us to a few other couples who were her long-time friends. In the evenings, we rotated hosting dinners.

Salisbury is where Andrew Jackson studied law, and Daniel Boone's family lived. From 5:00 to 9:00 pm every Friday in spring, the town had a Night Out. That meant shops and restaurants painted kids' faces, gave roses to moms, and offered free apple pie bites, candy, and balloons. Free band music set in motion spontaneous dancing in the streets. Every second Saturday was a Studio Crawl, a walking tour of artists' studios, an overflow from Charlotte where the cost of living was much higher. Around the town were two dozen pieces of public art. Could this big-city girl live in a small American town like this?

We found a wine cellar in the basement of an old building. While Bill tasted local wines, I got lost on a whole floor of antiques and collectibles. Tucked among other treasures was a three-foot-tall ornament tree! For only $11, it had hooks for thirty-two pieces of our Christmas ornament collection. Then, from the shelves of a Goodwill Store we spotted a huge Wowee RoboReptile dinosaur that was for auction the following Tuesday. My knight won it for my grandson in Canada for only $5. I was thrilled until I found out how much it cost to ship it!

Charlotte, NC (population 700,000) is the largest financial center in the United States, next to New York City, because it is home to the Bank of America headquarters. At the end of the free trolley rides at the Fourth Ward, we leisurely explored restored Victorian era homes and establishments. There was also the National Whitewater Center, an Olympics training site. But we loved most the Billy Graham Library. Flowered pathways led to a brown barn-like building

the Billy Graham Library

with a fifty-foot cross-shaped door/window. Inside were his religious · works and other religious items. It was a beautifully serene place, a welcome retreat from all our touring around.

From Charlotte, we drove to Sea Grove. It is a unique community of about a hundred potters clustered around four roads. We learned various techniques of glazing pottery: dipping, pouring, brushing, sponging, and spraying. One pot cost $2,500 (reputedly, a quarter of Atlanta prices). In the Great White Oak Gallery, one red Asian-inspired pot stood out from the rest, especially with a much lower price. We thought it would fit perfectly in Trisha's Zen-inspired home. We just hoped it wouldn't break before we got to Seattle since we didn't know when that might be.

Driving the Blue Ridge Parkway

In our last three weeks, we camped at the TT Green Mountain RV Park in Lenoir, North Carolina. Nearby, the Blue Ridge Parkway was celebrating its 75th year. It runs along the famous Blue Ridge of the Appalachian Mountains. The southern terminus is at Mile Post (MP) 469 on the boundary of the Great Smoky Mountains National Park near Asheville, North Carolina. It starts at MP 0 at the Shenandoah National Park in Virginia. Driving through would have taken about ten to twelve hours, nonstop. After surfing the Net, reading brochures, and talking to people, we drew up a plan to cover the Parkway in three separate legs.

The first stop on our first leg was Blowing Rock. The town got its name from wind currents that blow air vertically up the gorge, causing light objects, like leaves or snow, to float upwards. According to legend, two lovers were on the rock when the man received a notice to go into battle. He became so conflicted that he threw himself into the valley, but the woman prayed to the Great Spirit, and a gust of wind blew the man back up. We were also drawn to Grandfather Mountain, famous for The Mile High Swinging Bridge built to give visitors a breathtaking view from Linville Peak. Mr. Adventurer crossed the bridge; I didn't. From the Linn Cove Visitors' Center, there was a stunning view of the Linn Cove Viaduct, a 1,243-foot concrete segmental bridge that snaked around Grandfather Mountain, the Parkway's last section completed in 1983.

The second leg of our drive through the Parkway started, just like a normal day, from Asheville, North Carolina. Craggy Gardens would have been spectacular had the rhododendrons been in full bloom (which happens in late June to early August). Shrubs as tall as full-grown trees lined the Parkway. Then we climbed the 6,700-foot Mt. Mitchell, the highest peak on the East Coast. Halfway to the observation tower, my heart began pounding hard. Soon I was so completely out of breath that I had to stop. I was years younger than Bill but, at 62, I began to feel a lot older! We decided to get back to

camp for some needed rest and let whiz by Crabtree Meadows, Little'
Switzerland, and the North Carolina Mining Museum. Our last stop
was at Linville Falls, cascading down from the Linville Peak of
Grandfather Mountain, a drop of 2,000 feet.

Our last leg consisted of a three-day drive through the Virginia
Section of the Parkway. Day 1 started with the Blue Ridge Music Center

our photo of Mabry Mill

and the Peaceful Hearts
Alpacas where we ordered
a customized winter hat
for me. When we chanced
upon the Puckett Cabin,
it was quite fascinating to
learn about Orlean Hawks
Puckett, famous midwife of
the late 1800s. Legend has
it that she assisted in giving
birth, for $1 per baby, to
about a thousand infants in
fifty years (she lived to be 102). Ironically, not one of her twenty-four
children survived beyond infancy! But when we reached the most
photographed and painted Mabry Mill, we were in awe. Incomparable
beauty was created by the perfectly positioned and proportioned
mill, pond, and plants.

On Day 2 we arrived in Roanoke, Virginia, a charming mountain
city of 300,000, much like Baguio in the Philippines, although not
as congested. After dinner at an Italian restaurant in Central Square,
on our way back to our motel, I saw a big star shining from atop one
of the hills. It was the Roanoke Star, the world's largest freestanding
illuminated man-made star, constructed in 1949 at the top of Mill
Mountain! It stands 88.5 feet tall with 2,000 feet of neon tubing that
requires 17,500 watts. It started as white, became red, white, and blue
for six years after the Twin Towers Attack, then all white again after
the Virginia Tech massacre. Now it turns red whenever there is a
traffic fatality, a unique and special way to mourn collectively as a city.

Day 3 started with a short drive to the Peaks of Otter: Sharp Top,
Flat Top, and Harkening Hill. A hike up Sharp Top would have taken
around three hours, so we just took pictures from the Peaks of Otter
Lodge. Besides, Bill's real interest was Poplar Forest, the summer

retreat of Thomas Jefferson and his home after the British drove him away from Monticello in 1781. Completely balanced in design and octagonal in shape, that was where he found peace in his writings and thoughts. I hope to find my own Poplar Forest someday.

Our next stop was the Natural Bridge, a continuing work of art carved by Cedar Creek for the past 500 million years. US Route 11 runs on top of it. Just below the bridge, the letters GW (George Washington?) are inscribed about twenty-three feet above the stream's surface. It was worth the over-priced admission fee even if a low-quality wax museum and an almost empty toy store were tucked into the experience. But we spent so much time there that we arrived in Lexington way past the open hours of the only home of Stonewall Jackson. He was the Confederate general accidentally killed by one of his men. Some say that the Confederacy would have won, had he not died, and America, as we know it, would not be the same as it is today. We visited the Virginia Military Institute instead where a large statue honors him.

It was already past 6:00 pm and our GPS indicated we would be back at the campground in four hours. It was another long, tiring day. But I was proud that we had explored the Blue Ridge Parkway well. After all the driving, it felt good to be "home." This word had come to mean, not a state, not a city, not a street, but where the RV happened to be parked.

Green Mountain RV Park is what I would call a Nature RV Resort that suited the sightseeing *cum* relaxing Option 3 of RVing. (Please see Appendix 6 for the Four Kinds of Campgrounds). Each site had a big wooden deck for enjoying the outdoors and entertaining friends. A small stream flowing at the back of our site gave us soothing, relaxing sounds at night. Many tall trees shaded most of the Resort and a little lake up the hill beyond the Clubhouse was available for fishing. This campground also featured a nine-hole golf course, so we bought our starter golf clubs. Every Friday evening was a free concert/ dance. On Memorial Day, a couple taught us how to dance the East Coast Swing, and a new dance got added to our repertoire!

Finally, we were indeed cruising. We had equipped ourselves with an upgraded Thousand Trails Membership, a Class A motorhome, and little red Saturn. We finally had what we needed to do it all. It would be hard to forget our two-month stay in North Carolina. But we were raring to go further north to do more cruising!

PART 2

Meeting Challenges

"We shall not cease from exploration, and the end of all our exploring will be to arrive where we started and know the place for the first time."
T. S. Eliot

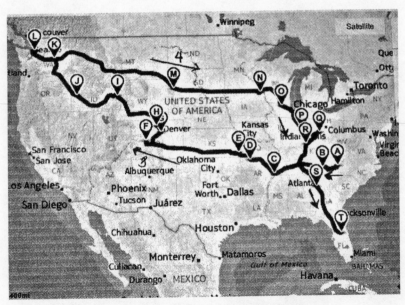

our second and third cross-continent runs

Chapter 9: Having to Turn West

North Carolina, Tennessee, and Arkansas, United States
June–July 2009

Even the best-laid plans can remain just that: plans. It was July, and we were all set to continue up north to escape the summer heat in the Southeast and to catch the spectacle of fall in the Northeast. We had to turn west, however, like many others centuries before us, to look for "gold." I had to go back because moving forward would not get me where I wanted to be.

As soon as I reached five years as a permanent resident in the United States, I had applied for citizenship. It was on my own merit, having divorced my first American husband. I also did not want to take advantage of Trisha's citizenship, even if that path would have been easier. Back then, I did not have a bit of hesitation to go RVing across the country. My lawyer assured me that any Commission on Immigration Services (CIS) office equipped to do so could do the next step in the process, fingerprinting. Tough luck! We got the forwarded mail a day after the fingerprinting appointment. Many have warned me that I should never ignore a directive from the CIS, or it might be interpreted as disinterest and become a reason for a denial.

My son-in-law in Seattle regularly forwarded our mail to us. Unfortunately, a batch of letters came a day after we had left our friend's house in Fort Myers. Instead of being forwarded to our next resort, it got sent back to Seattle. After tracing it through different resorts we had been to, we finally got it a couple of months later. I lost the time to find a proper office where I could have done the fingerprinting and missed the appointment date altogether! I had to appeal my case personally. Besides, I needed to be in Seattle for the written test and the final interview.

On the first week of September, Cristine was also getting married in Alaska. Flying there from Seattle made sense. In mid-August, there would also be another reunion of Bill's close high school friends in Crested Butte, Colorado, and that would be kind of on the way. Christmas with Trisha likewise sounded great; I would finally be able to give her that red pot from Sea Grove. And if my appeal succeeded, we could also visit April and my eldest sister Cynthia in Manila. If we left right away, we would have more than two months with time for some brief stops!

Our first such stop was at the most visited national park in the country, the Great Smoky Mountains National Park. Only two of its ten campgrounds could accommodate the size of our RV. We stayed at Elkmont near the Park Headquarters on the Tennessee side. There were no hookups, so we had to dry camp. Luckily, I survived the next four days!

Others said a trail led to fireflies that blink synchronously, but we did not have the luxury of time, so we limited ourselves to the most popular spots in the Park. Cades Cove gave us a view of old Appalachian life and plenty of wildlife sightings. The state line between North Carolina and Tennessee ran through the center at Newfound Gap where the Rockefeller Memorial stands. From there, we saw how the serene morning scene changed in the afternoon to one with feathers of fog rising from the canopy of trees, which is why the Park is called the Great Smokies.

All around the Park, within a half to an hour drive are fascinating towns. Just outside the Park's eastern entrance is Asheville in North Carolina where its jewel, Biltmore Estate, was built by George Vanderbilt II. It is the largest privately owned home in America with 250 rooms in 175,000 square feet on 8,000 acres of gardens, vegetable patches, and orchards. Estate staff told us that Christmas was an awesome time to be there, but it would be too cold for me.

Between Asheville and the Oconaluftee Visitors Center at the eastern entrance to the Park, we discovered Cherokee, North Carolina and the Cherokee Indian Reservation, headquarters of the Eastern Band. The city has many historical reminders of the Trail of Tears that began there when the 1830 Indian Removal Act forcibly relocated American Indians to the west. Now there is a bustling tourism industry around the Native-American owned Harrah's Cherokee Casino, a scene oft-repeated all over the country. At places like this, memories of the early controversial treatment of American Indians stand side-by-side with symbols of their current "redemption."

Passing through Tennessee and Arkansas

At the western end is Gatlinburg, Tennessee, a touristy city in the foothills of the Pisgah National Forest. Hotel, entertainment, and shopping chains co-exist with flowing streams, wildflower beds, and green hillsides. Just next door in Pigeon Forge is Dollywood, Dolly Parton's theme park. No child would get bored there; *I* would never get bored there. It has three outlet malls! Bill got us out of there fast but not before I had bought a new pair of shoes. The area quickly disappeared from our list of places to settle; a one-bedroom condo costs a hefty $600,000!

At Oak Ridge, Tennessee, Jim, one of Bill's close high school friends gave us a glimpse of the decommissioning of the vast central production facilities of the Manhattan Project. His career included such projects as the cleaning up of the Three-Mile Island nuclear reactor disaster. From the top of a hill, he pointed to a building with a 43-hectare footprint and five million square feet of four floors. After a quick tour of Oak Ridge, Jim took us to his Knoxville home and played for us 'The Secret City," a documentary of how the town kept the "big secret." We would complete the picture of this Project that changed the course of WWII in Washington and New Mexico.

In Nashville, we caught the last day of the Country Music Awards (CMA) Music Festival. Taylor Swift was signing autographs inside Bridgestone Arena where her huge, expensive, fancy RV (putting ours to shame) was parked at the center. At an oversized tent in front of the CMA Music Hall of Fame, Martina McBride was holding a Country Stars' Auction. American Idol finalist Bo Bice, for whom I voted, could only stay atop for two seconds

Taylor Swift's RV at Bridgestone Arena

at the Celebrity Bull Riding Challenge Tent. Other country stars were performing at the Riverfront Park and on the Chevy Stage at 30-minute intervals. On the other side of the Cumberland River at the big LP field, more stars performed before sold-out crowds in the evenings. Sports, Family, and Fun Zones occupied four blocks lined with kiosks giving away freebies of many American favorites.

But it was a blazing HOT Sunday at 95°F made worse by the infamous Tennessee humidity. By 5:00 pm, I couldn't breathe and couldn't continue walking. We sought refuge at a boots store, but the owner kept staring at us. Luckily, I made it to the air-conditioned public library where I was able to sit down and rest. We heard that some were rushed to the hospital for heat strokes, but why me? I had flourished in that kind of climate for fifty-four years!

After a night of rest in the RV, I felt much better for another view of Nashville. The legacy of Andrew Jackson, America's seventh President, was the annexation of Arkansas and Michigan. His home, "The Hermitage," was exceptionally appealing, especially the memorial to his wife who died just weeks before he claimed the presidency. Her death was believed to have been brought about by the opposition's exposé that they had wed even before her divorce had been finalized. It was a brazen attempt to overcome his overwhelming popularity as the general who turned the tide in the War of 1812, which England had waged to regain control of the country. Politics can be cruel.

In Columbia, quite close to Nashville, is the ancestral home of James Polk, the eleventh President. He led the country to victory in the Mexican-American War, and the annexation of the rest of the West became his legacy. He died just three months after the end of his first and only term. Sickly from the start, it is believed that the hard work he put in cost him his life. Two paintings done only two years apart clearly showed how much he had aged. Once in a while you find really competent political leaders. I secretly hoped the Philippines could find one!

Close to our campground, TT Natchez Trace Wilderness Preserve, was the town of Hohenwald. Meriwether Lewis, the leader of the Lewis and Clark Expedition, died there in mysterious circumstances (syphilis or suicide or both?). An uncompleted monument stands above his burial site, near the roadhouse where he died, symbolizing a great life that was cut tragically short. It was too bad we didn't have time to explore the Natchez Trace Parkway linking Mississippi, Alabama, and Tennessee. We promised ourselves that we would, on the way back.

An "Old Order" Amish community thrives in Lawrenceburg, at Tennessee's Etheridge Area. We marveled at their crafts and produce at the delightful Yoder's Homestead Market. Many Amish migrated to

Amish horse-drawn carriages

America in the early eighteenth century after a schism in Switzerland led by Jakob Ammann. In the 1860s, the conservative faction withdrew from the wider body and reemphasized simple living, plain dressing, and refusal to adopt modern conveniences. It was fascinating to see them up close, but when I attempted to take a photo, an Amish mother motioned me away. We were bound to encounter more of them, however. A study at Ohio State University indicates that there are about 270,000, most of them distributed in eighteen states.

When we reached Memphis, the RV's front air conditioning unit failed in the blistering humid 97-degree heat. We had to go to Camping World at Little Rock, Arkansas to get it fixed. That gave us time only for a peek at Elvis' home in Graceland; his plane named Lisa Marie, his blue El Dorado convertible, "The Elvis Presley Boulevard" sign, and the Heartbreak Hotel.

We had time for one tour, though, and chose the Sun Studios tour. Our very entertaining guide told of the careers of Johnny Cash, Carl Perkins, Jerry Lee Lewis, and Elvis Presley while playing outtakes from actual sessions. One December night, the microphones had been accidentally left on during a playful jam session of the four friends. The rollicking play *Million Dollar Quartet*, which Bill and I had seen in Seattle, memorialized this heartwarming incident.

The repair of our motorhome's AC in Little Rock took two days, giving us some time to go around town. We found these beautiful words, "dedicated to the idea that people need to make connections in this world," at a marker near the Big Dam Bridge. It is the longest pedestrian bridge in the world at 4,226 linear feet. We also visited the Bill Clinton Presidential Library that stands adjacent to the Arkansas River, and the handsome old bridge that spans it. At the Capitol, we were greeted by the Little Rock Nine, symbol of desegregation in the state, honoring nine African-American students who were refused attendance at the local high school.

One day at the Etheridge area, I felt a terrible pain in my lower right abdomen. No, it wasn't appendicitis, but it lingered for a good hour. We wondered if the anxiety over my application for citizenship and being constantly on the go again were bringing back my old friend Stress. I was out of breath at Grandfather Mountain, melted down in Nashville, then this! I had also begun to have difficulty falling asleep readily and tended to wake up several times throughout the night. We installed blackout curtains yet the problems persisted. I worried about the impact on my health of sleeping less, which caused me to sleep less! The cycle became vicious. We decided to make a two-week stop in Bill's hometown in Kansas to consult a doctor. Waiting until Seattle might have been too long.

Chapter 10: Finding Time for a Few Stops

Missouri, Kansas, Colorado, Wyoming, Montana, Idaho, Washington, and Alaska, United States
July–September 2010

Bill's sister Rosemary and her husband Jack met us in Branson, Missouri before taking us to their hometown, Pittsburg, Kansas. Bill may be charming but Rosemary is all candy, sweet, thoughtful, and gracious. Jack is the perfect mate for her, a 100-per cent gentleman, an engineer, and model plane enthusiast. They treated me like a baby sister!

Branson has more than thirty shows at any one time. We chose to have dinner and see the show at "The Showboat," a 720-seat paddle boat on Table Rock Lake. It is the largest of its kind ever built on a fresh water lake. Near Branson is Silver Dollar City, built on top of Marvel Cave, a massive natural cavern where everyone who comes in has to crouch through four-foot-high narrow passageways. Unlike Disney famous for its rides, the City is dominated by shows.

Soon we were in Pittsburg (without the h). It was a busy mining town in the old days. Big Brutus, the second largest electric shovel in the world, is now sitting idle on the banks of an old mine pit. To cater to hungry miners, two miners' wives founded two chicken restaurants after the injury and death of their husbands. Sitting on their original locations half a mile from each other, Chicken Mary's and Chicken Annie's were featured in the "Kansas Fried Chicken War" on the Travel Channel. They give Pittsburg its reputation for the best fried chicken in the country. I believe Max's fried chicken in the Philippines can give them serious competition.

Our 37-foot motorhome fit perfectly in Jack's driveway. He ran a cord from a 30-amp outlet in his garage to give us power. We were happy neighbors for two weeks, the first time Bill and Rosemary were able to spend much time together since he left for college. I took the opportunity to consult Jack's doctor. While waiting for test results, we went on day trips together.

On the way to Tulsa, Oklahoma we visited the largest McDonald's store in the world. Stretching over the Will Rogers Turnpike, it covered about 30,000 square feet of space. A Will Rogers statue stood guard at the parking lot on each side of I-44. Vehicles bearing plates from almost every state filled both lots. I learned at the nearby Will Rogers Museum that the man was a regular presence in national events from 1879 until his life was cut short in a plane crash in 1926.

Just forty-five minutes from the Dock home, we found the biggest continuously flowing waterfall in the state. It is close to Joplin, Missouri, the city that would be devastated by a massive tornado a year later. Grand Falls is also called the "Little Niagara." The city also takes pride in the George Washington Carver National Monument. Carver worked on the promotion of alternative crops to cotton, such as peanuts (more than 300 ways) and sweet potatoes (more than 100 applications). In 1941 *Time* magazine dubbed him the "Black Leonardo," undermining the widespread stereotype that the black are intellectually inferior. I felt he did that for all minorities.

A few miles beyond Joplin in Carthage, Missouri is the Precious Moments Chapel and Garden. Artist and creator Samuel J. Butcher used his well-known Precious Moments messengers to bring to life stories from the Bible in dozens of murals, covering nearly 5,000 square feet in the chapel and more in the garden. I was proud when I found out on a bulletin board outside the chapel that the artist has retired and has chosen Cebu in southern Philippines as his home!

We also met Rosemary's children for dinner in Kansas City after tours of the Harley-Davidson plant and the Hallmark Cards factory. Back in Pittsburg, we found out that all my test results were negative. I was puzzled but felt relieved so we bid Rosemary and Jack goodbye. We took one last look at the great Kansas plains, the herds of cattle, the isolated small oil rigs on vast fields of wheat. I wondered when we would again see low-flying crop dusters and dwarfed motorcycles on empty highways. We stopped in Salina, Kansas for another night at a Walmart.

Making Other Stops

We brought the RV to a storage facility in Denver and drove to Crested Butte for another reunion of Bill's close high school friends. Mt. Crested Butte rises to more than 12,000 feet above sea level (the town's elevation is about 8,800 feet). On our hike to its summit, I couldn't make it to the top, and I was the youngest in the group! At about every hundred steps, I had to take "breathtaking" stops. Just at the timberline before the alpine tundra, I had to stay behind at the rest area to feed the chipmunks and to be fed to the mosquitoes. I needed a second opinion in Seattle.

Hiking the adjoining hills ablaze with colorful wildflowers (Crested Butte is the wildflower capital of Colorado) proved more doable. We also took a walking tour of the town. When the group braved a whitewater adventure, the hydrophobic Carol (even if I had come from a 7,107-island archipelago) stayed home to write. But when the entire town gathered at the Summer Music Festival, the grass-covered ground proved to be a large enough dance hall for Bill and me!

From Crested Butte, we made a short visit to Bill's daughter Suzanne and family in Denver. We got to watch some good tennis matches before camping for a couple of days at the Rocky Mountain National Park, just north of the city. With a median elevation of 10,000 feet (Long's Peak is the highest at 14,400 feet), it makes Colorado the "highest" state even before it legalized marijuana. We looked for our campground from the south entrance to the north and finally found it near the Visitors' Center, a stunning legacy of the famous architect Frank Lloyd Wright.

Though we were on a strict timetable, we could not resist stopping by two more must-see national parks. Besides, they were kind of on the way. Even without any reservations (the system is first come, first served) we were lucky that we were given five nights at the Grand Tetons

view of the Grand Tetons, from a stream

National Park and, later, four nights at Yellowstone National Park.

A fifty-mile mountain range that sprang up when the Teton fault moved and sank the valley below into Jackson Hole, the Tetons has no foothills, making the pointed peaks more dramatic. There are three that are close together: the Grand Teton (highest at 13,770 feet), the Middle Teton, and the South Teton. French fur traders must have longed for those elegant shapes and named them "tetons," French for female breasts! Even if I had never traded fur and I wasn't male, I found them incredibly spectacular. A little further removed are the most pointed Mt. Teewinot and Mt. Moran, with its glacier that looks like a skillet.

On our first day, we attended sessions with the park rangers to learn more about the area. Over the next two days, we took the self-guided tour of the park, stopping at all the overlooks and turnouts for different shots of the majestic sight. At the Chapel of Transfiguration, a large window makes a veritable altar of the view. Jenny Lake had a more intimate setting, but Jackson Lake Lodge offered a panoramic view of Willow Flats where there were plenty of wildlife. When we were driving past herds of cattle, Bill said, "watch carefully, sometimes others graze with them." Soon pronged antelope appeared, followed by elk, then bison. At Hayden and Lamar Valleys, hundreds of bison created huge traffic jams. Grizzly bears, wolves, coyotes, mule deer, and elk were all around in this place. No wonder we call it the Serengeti of North America!

On the way to Yellowstone, the first national park created in 1872, boiling springs were all along West Thumb on the shores of Yellowstone Lake, the largest mountain lake in North America. Signs of the fifty devastating fires of 1988 were still very evident. Just as we had anticipated, we had our second-anniversary dinner at the Inn beside Old Faithful that gushes every ninety minutes, sometimes to as high as 150 feet. Around him are five hundred of the 900 geysers in the world. They were in Black Sand Basin, Biscuit Basin, Upper, Middle and Lower Basins, and a little farther up north at Porcelain, Back, and Monument Basins.

The Park sits atop a subterranean volcano, three to seven miles below the caldera that formed after it erupted 640,000 years ago. It is home to the tallest geyser in the world Steamboat at 400 feet, mud pots (Mud Volcano), steam vents (Black Growler), and colorful hot springs including the Grand Prismatic Spring. Another spectacle is the 380-foot Lower Falls (taller than Niagara Falls) on the stunning Artist Point, an overlook of Yellowstone's Grand Canyon. In the northern end of the Park is Mammoth Hot Springs. It is a living sculpture of travertine terraces, carved over a thousand years from the interaction of transferred magma heat and deep pockets of water from snowmelt and rain that seep through fissures.

We did not regret spending nine days at Grand Tetons and Yellowstone. They both offer lodges, inns, cabins, RV campgrounds,

and tent villages from which to base an exploration. Each village has a general store, service station, dining facilities, and other amenities. Only a few had internet facilities, however, so I was not able to keep up with my blog and social media postings. But I knew I

Grand Prismatic Spring, minus the colors

would have lots of time for that in Seattle.

After passing through Wyoming and Montana, we arrived in Boise, Idaho to visit Bill's son Jim and family. We parked at a campground near their home. One day they stayed overnight with us. On our last night, however, the RV rocked from the tremendous seventy mph rain-free wind that swept Boise, rendering the whole area powerless until morning. When we had approached the area from the east, we also met a blinding dust storm. I prayed I would not encounter a tornado!

From Boise, Idaho, we crossed the Blue Mountains and settled in TT Moses Lake Resort in Moses Lake, Washington. The unusual topography of the eastern part of the state is widely believed to be the result of massive ice floods from Lake Missoula in Montana that carried 520 million cubic meters of water. Imagine the power of that much water rushing to the ocean in just three days! We visited the Grand Coulee Dam, currently the largest dam in North America and the fourth-largest in the world. On the way to the dam, we spotted the medicinal Soap Lake filled with what looked like soap suds. Summer Falls was an oasis, a 165-foot waterfall created by the releasing of water from the dam. Most intriguing was Dry Falls, once the biggest waterfall in the world, double Niagara but without water. But the highlight of our stop was the Hanford Reach National Monument south of Moses Lake at the outlying delta of the Columbia River. Seven reactors were built there to produce plutonium for the WWII atomic bombs. I finally saw the second piece of the Manhattan Project. The third and last part would be in New Mexico.

After reaching Seattle, we stored the RV and flew to Alaska for Cristine's wedding. We hadn't thought we would be back in Alaska so soon, but Cristine had found her soulmate. As soon as we arrived, we rented an RV and parked it in her driveway. In over a year, we had hoped to see moose and that afternoon a mother and her calf were right there in her backyard! When the couple left for their honeymoon, we took Bill's grandson Kyle, who had come for the wedding, RVing in Soldotna/Kenai and Seward. Those towns were just slightly off the same road we took to Homer the previous year. Eight-and-a-half miles west of Seward lies the famous Exit Glacier. It is so named because it had receded about two miles, still counting, since 1815. I finally braved a glacier walk, but it felt like being in a freezer, so I ran back to the RV as fast as I could!

After Kyle went back to Hawaii and the soggy weather changed, we hurried to Talkeetna for another chance to see Mt. McKinley. And we finally got to see the Mighty One! It is necessary to point out that, although there are 650 higher peaks in the Himalayas and forty-four in South America, McKinley rises all alone from a sea-level base. She looked massively spectacular! It was truly quite a sight, one other stop worth making.

Chapter 11: Waiting in Washington

Washington, United States
September 2010–February 2011

As soon as we got back in Seattle, I found out that the CIS had approved my appeal for a new fingerprinting appointment. Unfortunately, the day they gave me coincided with a scheduled mini family reunion in Spokane, Washington. The city is on the Spokane River 429 miles south of Calgary and 270 miles east of Seattle, quite accessible for Claudine, Trisha, and their families. Luckily, there was an office there that could do fingerprinting!

There was a lot to see in Spokane. The city hosted the first environmentally-themed world's fair in Expo '74," the smallest city yet to host one. The fairgrounds transformed downtown into a hundred acre Riverfront Park with a giant red wagon and other giant playthings, a Clock Tower, and a 1906 carousel. Rides under a netted cityscape, a cluster sculpture of runners depicting the annual Daffodil Run, and a Sky Ride that takes you to the Spokane Falls in the heart of the city have also remained. At the well-maintained K/M Ponderosa Falls campground, the kids enjoyed trick-or-treating, basketball, mini-golf, the pool, and the arcade. The couples rotated cooking and dishwashing duties at the clubhouse and playing games at either of the two cabins we had rented.

The fingerprinting, however, was a disaster! The Immigration Officer advised me to apply corn huskers' oil for a month before coming back for another try. The only thing I could think of doing was to sell my services as murderer-for-hire and have no fear of getting caught because there will be no forensic evidence that would connect me to the crime! They say Asians are most susceptible to this condition. But I was only too glad to pass my dishwashing duties to Bill!

While waiting for my next appointment, a friend who worked at Microsoft treated us to an "intimate" tour of the office complex in Redmond, Washington. Fides had managed the operations team at I/ACT while I handled the marketing group. That put us right in each other's paths, amid the usual conflict between such groups in any company. But fate brought us together again in Seattle where we became good friends. She and her husband had also visited with us in San Jose, California, and Spokane, Monroe and Bellingham, Washington.

We had lunch at The Commons and visited the Microsoft Museum where we had our photo taken with the "Founders." The Microsoft Campus is a decentralized, 300-acre corporate park with approximately 40 buildings housing 14,000 offices. There are over 78,000 employees in a total of fifteen million square feet in 127 sites. In my entire career in the IT industry, I never got the chance to work with this corporate giant. It would have been an honor.

Fides also took us to the opening of The Microsoft Store in the posh Bel-Square Mall in Bellevue. It was only the seventh such store in the country at the time. With Fides' employee discount, Bill bought a brand new 3-lb.Toshiba Protégé for my birthday and Kinect promo bundles as Christmas gifts for our kids' families. We finished Christmas shopping in an instant!

Then Mother Nature decided it would be a White Thanksgiving. Record snowfall blanketed the TT Thunderbird Resort in Monroe, forcing us to cancel a traditional turkey dinner and my birthday night

out. Management could not risk their pipes freezing, so we scrimped on the reserved fresh water in our tank. We still had power but, with very little propane left, we had to confine ourselves to meals cooked in the microwave or the electric skillet.

a white Thanksgiving

When the snow cleared, we went to pick up some medicine at Walgreens. At the free blood pressure monitor, I was curious and took my blood pressure. It was 160/85! I should have seen Bill's doctor as soon as I got to Seattle. Yes, I had signs of early hypertension. We had to change our eating habits, and I had to take a small dose of a diuretic and a baby aspirin daily. I have since dropped the aspirin because I thought it brought me a lot of hyperacidity.

But I was happy to get a new fingerprinting appointment. The bad news: it was again a disaster! The good news: a second rejection automatically meant a waiver, according to the Officer. I just had to wait for a final disposition of my case. Since we knew it would probably take longer, I wanted to go south to look for warmer weather.

Looking for Warmer Weather

We found the Chehalis RV Resort, the campground where TT started, close enough to Seattle (two-hour drive) and south enough to matter. As soon as we had hooked up, we put up our usual Christmas decoration. Interesting sights surrounded our campground. Yard Birds, initially a military surplus store started in 1947, had become a large complex with shops, a full-service grocery, and a Christmas crafts fair. A large black bird with a yellow beak (a la Heckle and Jeckle) sits in the yard. Then we found the Mima Mounds, looking like pimples on a prairie, ranging from 3 to 50 meters in diameter, 30 centimeters to 2 meters in height, and up to 50 per hectare in density. I understand they can be found in other parts of the country, too.

But much of the campground was closed for the season. The woodsy setting is probably best in the spring, summer and fall. There must have been just ten of us in the small area that was left open. Of the amenities, only the spa and sauna were available. There was even a flood scare from a Chehalis River overflow. We transferred to a campground in nearby Elma where Texas Hold 'Em and a billiards tournament entertained us almost every night.

At the start of the holiday season, we drove to Seattle for my grandson's birthday party only to get another bad news from the CIS. A letter stated that, since I had studied the automation of the US internal revenue system under a US IRS grant, I should be in the Philippines implementing what I learned. A World Bank loan and US AID grant had funded the automation of a similar system in the country. The Philippines' Bureau of Internal Revenue replied that I had completed the system as Deputy Commissioner a decade ago. I waited for the judgment, worrying no end.

We thought we could tour around Elma while waiting, especially since for the first time in many days, sunlight swept over southwestern Washington. Although it was forecast to be only a high of 43°F, we seized the rare Northwest opportunity and drove our little red Saturn west towards the coast where the Pacific meets the southern tip of the Olympic Peninsula. We went south to the Cranberry Coast. Bill was thoroughly amused as I kept humming, "let me take you down where I'm going to ...*cranberry* fields forever."

The first town on the Cranberry Coast is Markham. Ocean Spray brings all the cranberries to this town, processes them, and distributes craisins (dried cranberries) to different parts of the country. Driving south on Highway 105, we reached Grayland, site of the Annual Cranberry Festival where nearly 150 years ago, Finnish farmers cultivated cranberries in bright red berry bogs that have become tourist attractions. North Cove's claim to fame is Washaway Beach, a two-mile stretch that has been clawed away by the Pacific Ocean since 1891. There were sentimental objects left on the beach and homes were hanging half off the cliff shore. South Bend on Willapa Bay, dubbed the "Fresh Oyster Capital of the World," is the source of 15 percent of the oysters consumed in the country. Mountains of oyster shells were all over town, sights I had also seen around Manila Bay. At the end of the loop back towards Elma and a little north of South Bend is the town of Raymond. A Wildlife-Heritage Sculpture Corridor of 200 enchanting steel sculptures of wildlife and people is along Highway 101, State Route 6, and throughout downtown. Local artists designed and installed the corridor in 1993, perhaps with something like the Filipino *Bayanihan* spirit, or communal unity and cooperation.

The next sunny day saw us driving to the Pacific Ocean again, this time going north. At the town of Aberdeen, we saw the largest compass in the world (forty feet in diameter) at the intersection of the Chehalis and Wishkah rivers. Hidden inside a humble muffler repair shop, we stumbled upon a statue of Kurt Cobain, the work of the owner's wife. Cobain, leader of the multiplatinum grunge band Nirvana, was born in Aberdeen but, because of his use of dangerous drugs, was banned from the town. He moved to neighboring Hoquiam where, at twenty-seven, a year after the birth of his love child with Courtney Love of The Hole, he fired a shotgun into his mouth. Not far from these two towns, where the Chehalis River meets the mighty Pacific, is Ocean Shores, a touristy strip of real estate. All the fire hydrants were bright yellow, instead of the usual red. A huge yellow propane tank had Betty Boop eyes painted on it. The roof of a fishing boat relic left on the street was also yellow. I love the color yellow; Ocean Shores is my kind of town!

On the way back to our home in Elma, we caught a glimpse of Nuclear Plants 4 and 5 of the WPPSS (Washington Public Power Supply System). Mothballed at a cost of $2.25 billion, they are now called "whoops." I smiled because the Philippines had a similar fiasco, the mothballed Bataan Nuclear Power Plant of the Marcos regime.

Getting Things Together

Still there was no news. As expected, Christmas and New Year's Eves were spent with Trisha and her family. We had the traditional *Noche Buena,* good old holiday ham, *queso de bola*, whole wheat *pan de sal*, and thick Spanish hot chocolate for each night. Trisha finally got her red pot from Sea Grove. Back at Elma, members, of what Bill calls my "Estrogen" Book Club, and their spouses drove all the way from Seattle to share a holiday potluck with us.

My blog got a great deal of attention. I worked out the theme and layout, edited and uploaded photos, and wrote posts. This investment in time and effort paid off when fellow bloggers in the now defunct Entrecard gave me two awards: Most Stylish Blog and Most Versatile Blog. It was getting more and more conceivable that a book could be next!

We also thought it wise to start counseling sessions with John, pastoral counselor in a West Seattle parish, since we had begun to have misunderstandings. Bill and John had been friends since they met at the Parish where John worked and where Bill was a member of the pastoral council. We had several dialogs. He coached us to be cautious of the cultural divide between us, magnified by our age and the cramped living arrangements in an RV. Through Skype, John would be available to us anytime and anywhere we needed him as we continued our travels

When February came, I got an invitation from the CIS for the Big Day! I had been feverishly reviewing for the written test with the guidebook they provided and trying all versions of sample tests on their website. It was no surprise to me that I had zero mistakes! When the Immigration Officer turned to the oral interview, he quickly realized I knew a lot about America. Fascinated by my stories of RVing, he said, "You should write a book!" In short, my appeal got the nod. I had gone back to the Northwest to look for "gold" and got it. Some things are worth waiting for, however long the wait. On Valentine's Day 2011, fifty-four of us from twenty-six countries took our oath of allegiance to the country that welcomed us, whatever our dreams might have been.

taking my oath as a US citizen

Right after the day of the ceremony, Bill had the RV roof replaced, due to leaks we discovered, at Camping World in Fife, Washington. Then we stored the RV at his friend's spacious backyard in Sumner, Washington and flew to the Philippines for a three-month vacation in the tropical isles. It was my first trip outside the country as a US citizen!

Chapter 12: Rounding Out the Great Plains

Montana, South Dakota, North Dakota, Nebraska, Kansas, and Iowa, United States
June–July 2011

When we got back from the Philippines, we had all of six months to get to Florida for the winter. We only had two months to cross the country from Florida to Seattle the year before. We could continue the kind of cruising we had started in North Carolina. We had a chance to be happily surprised by what we see and to linger a bit more if we liked what we saw. Robert Louis Stevenson once said, "I travel not to go anywhere, but to go. I travel for travel's sake. The great affair is to move." And move in a truly cruising pace.

First we met Claudine and family at Glacier National Park which was just a three to four-hour drive from Calgary. When we were about to leave Seattle, we discovered that the RV had water and propane heating issues. There were no available slots at Camping World in Fife but, when we got to Spokane, a shop fixed our water problem, but not the heating. That night, lows of 39°F felt a lot colder because of 20–30 mph winds, even if we were all bundled in thick double blankets. The next day, we had to transfer to the KOA campground that had electric hookups.

Established in 1910, Glacier National Park spans 16,000 square miles shared by Canada and the United States. Six of the glacier-topped mountains are above 10,000 feet, many above 9,000, and more above 8,000. Right on the border, Chief Mountain stands at 9,008 feet of solid rectangular rock in the middle of vast empty plains. We drove a lot through the Going-to-the-Sun Road, itself an engineering wonder with fifty miles of scenic mountain highway.

Of the estimated 150 originally found in the Park, there are only twenty-five glaciers left, and all of them are expected to be gone by 2030 if current global warming goes unabated. We may be doing our best to rescue wildlife from endangered status, but perhaps conserving glaciers is beyond human capability or will. We were glad to have found the time to visit the Park while it still thrived. The boys were happy to get Junior Ranger badges and to spot bears! But just like the glaciers, the boys were soon going, going, gone.

Next it was Jim and Suzanne and their families whom we met at Yellowstone. The North Entrance is six hours away from Glacier National Park, seven hours from Jim's in Boise and 10 ½ hours from Suzanne's in Denver. They rented a two-bedroom cabin, we camped nearby, and the kids thoroughly enjoyed the reunion. Yellowstone in spring looked very different. Snow still covered mountaintops; the colors seemed less vibrant, and the gushing less spectacular. Wildlife was not yet out grazing to stock up for the winter. Still, Old Faithful remained faithful. We even chanced upon Spasm Geyser that bursts out for thirty minutes every twelve hours.

After the mini-reunions, we were ready to round out the Great Plains. It is the breadbasket of the United States where the land is fertile and ideal for oats, wheat, corn, and now, soy. It reminds me of much smaller Central Luzon, the rice granary of the Philippines. The Plains is the most homogeneous (and monotonous) topography of any part of the United States with the greatest extremes in climate and the most tornadoes. It is, after all, the Land of Oz! Winters are cold, with frequent snowy blizzards, and summer temperatures can exceed 100°F!

Exploring North and South Dakota

We started with a three-week stay in Rapid City, South Dakota. As soon as we could, we rushed to Mt. Rushmore. The 60-foot faces of 465-foot-tall Washington, Jefferson, Roosevelt, and Lincoln, are the most solid memorial to American democracy I had ever seen. One visit was not

the Presidents and us

enough to bask in the feeling that Gutzon Borglum and a crew of 360 men created in fourteen years. Bill and I had to return for the moving night ritual for all American servicemen present.

When completed, it will be Crazy Horse that will be the world's largest sculpture. A memorial to the Lakota chief who defeated Custer in Billings, Montana, it will stand 641 feet long and 563 feet high. In 1929, A. Korczak, a Polish immigrant and former assistant to Borglum, had been commissioned by the Lakota Indian elders and after he had died, a foundation to complete the project was set up. Rapid City will then house the two monuments of the conflict between American Indians and European settlers and of great men who had built American democracy.

Leaving the Memorial, we spotted a sign that said, "Centermost Point in America." After following many arrows, we reached a compass rose marker surrounded by fifty state flags. America's Centermost Point is twenty miles north of Belle Fourche, South Dakota. According to Bill, this point was in Lebanon, Kansas before the addition of Alaska and Hawaii.

We explored South Dakota by taking day trips from our campground to landmarks around this center, an hour, maybe two or even three away. It's a good thing Bill likes to drive, not only to new places but even to old ones, as long as we take new routes. It's also a good thing I am small. Around the passenger seat are all those things I don't want to have to look for: laptop, camera, food, medicine, tissue box, hats, my purse, camera, sunglasses, etc. Whenever Bill pointed out some exciting scenery ahead, I hurried to grab the camera to take the shot. Sometimes I got frustrated by a dirty windshield but Bill did make it a point to clean it every time he filled up for gas. When I buried my head on the laptop, he listened to borrowed audio books from the library. That's when I would empty a huge bag of Cheetos in a jiffy! But there usually was a healthy partnership between us, unless and until my opinion differed with the GPS. That's when Bill gets stressed as he weighs the conflicting inputs. The GPS is now named Carmin (Carol and Garmin)!

Our first day trip was to the Badlands National Park, a hundred miles east of the Centermost Point. The Park preserves sharply eroded buttes, pinnacles, and spires blended with the largest protected mixed grass (with over twenty varieties) prairie in the United States. Even if the Park is surrounded by 50-mile-long cliff shelves, erosion continues at about an inch a year. Fossils are still begging to be found. As a matter of fact, a complete bone framework of a triceratops, a rhino-like beast the size of an elephant, is on exhibit at the Museum of Geology.

Mammoth Site in Hot Springs south of Rapid City is a sinkhole from which bones of fifty-nine mammoths were unearthed. Beside the NE Wyoming Visitors' Center is Vore Buffalo Jump, a sinkhole with bones of 20,000 buffalos. I think my grandsons would go wild in these places.

Sixty miles west of this Center, in northwestern Wyoming, is Devil's Tower, an igneous intrusion where magma from the Earth's mantle welled up between chunks of sedimentary rock. The Tower

was featured in the movie *"Close Encounters of the Third Kind."* Rising 5,112 feet above sea level, it challenges five thousand rock climbers each year. Indian legend has it that the tower surged higher and higher to protect eight kids from a giant bear's claws.

Devil's Tower

Sixty miles south of the Center is South Dakota's greener and higher Black Hills. On the highest points of the Hills, at Custer State Park, are Cathedral Spires, Needles' Eye, and other unique granite formations. The Black Hills were the first to be considered for the sculpture of the four presidents, but they eventually lost to Mt. Rushmore, Borglum's choice.

One hundred and fifty miles north of the Center, in North Dakota, is the least-visited among all national parks, the Theodore Roosevelt National Park. The conservationist President credited his success to his experiences at the Maltese Cross Cabin, preserved at the Visitors' Center. The Park's painted colors come from scoria, red rock produced from sediments of coal beds beneath, baked by lightning strikes and prairie fires that ignite them.

Before entering the Badlands, at the Eastern Entrance, is the Minuteman II Missile Historic Site. It is the first memorial to the Cold War erected after thousands of such sites were deactivated. It consists of Delta-01, the Launch Control Facility, and Delta-09, the Underground Silo. It is both sad and frightening that about five hundred of them can still be deployed in the United States. At the other end, the Western Entrance, is the Wall Drugstore. Ted Hustead, a 1929 pharmacy graduate, took his family to South Dakota and stumbled upon a tremendous marketing coup: free ice water for thirsty travelers! The complex has become a haven for tourists wanting everything Western. Today it still serves five thousand glasses of ice water a day.

We were surprised at everything the Rapid City area had to offer, including the Hart Ranch Camping Resort, a delightful campground we called home for three weeks. Two other South Dakota cities were also impressive. At Mitchell we toured the world's only Corn Palace. It has been rebuilt annually since 1882 using over 275,000 ears of twelve different colors of corn trimmed by grass, rye, wheat, etc. Further east is Sioux Falls where the flow of the Missouri River is broken by pink granite rocks, creating a superb system of small waterfalls right in the middle of the city.

Visiting Nebraska, Kansas, and Iowa

After South Dakota, we made a brief visit to Omaha, Nebraska where Bill had worked as District Technical Engineer for Caterpillar Tractor. He showed me the first house he ever bought and where his family lived when his three children were born. We were lucky that the owners graciously invited us in; it had changed little over the years. In Seattle, he had shown me four other homes where he had lived just like I showed him my four homes in Metro Manila.

There had been a swelling of the Missouri and Mississippi Rivers due to early snow melts and abundant rain. We didn't know what to expect. I was reminded of Manila floods when I saw entire sections of I-29 submerged in floodwaters. But here nature is again the culprit; in Metro Manila it had been waterways clogged with garbage. Still, we wanted to meet Rosemary and Jack and her children again. So we drove from Omaha to Kansas City. Ordinarily this trip would have taken three hours each way at the most. It took us four hours and fifteen minutes!

We took the RV to Camping World in Council Bluffs, Iowa to finally have the heating repaired. A magazine at the store featured a unique rotary jail that served the county from 1882 to 1969. While they were fixing the heating problem, we went to see what resembled an oversized bird cage with three floors, each housing ten cells. It was manually cranked to open to a cell for two (at times five were made to fit). The design only needed two guards. When it developed a tilt, it was classified as a death trap and was abruptly closed. I shuddered at the thought that people were incarcerated this way, like animals, with no hope of being reformed.

Within a four-hour round trip in Iowa were two other places worth the drive. First was the Bridges of Madison County in Winterset, Iowa, which was the setting of the movie where Clint Eastwood and Meryl Streep denied each other the love of their lives. I fell in love with those covered bridges (they used two in the movie). We even dined at the featured Northside Café. We also went to see the small and simple white cabin where the acting legend John Wayne was born. We could visit such places because we had all the time in the world. After all, we were tourists who were on the move to explore America, the beautiful.

Chapter 13: Becoming More than Tourists

Iowa, Minnesota, Illinois, Wisconsin, Indiana, and Ohio, United States
July–August 2011

G. K. Chesterton said, "The traveler sees what he sees. The tourist sees what he has come to see." That makes me turn a little red. I must confess that, after surfing the net, asking people, and perusing brochures, I always come up with a long list of places to see. But, after two years, some change eventually happened. We had become more than tourists; we had also become explorers, adventurers, and even pilgrims.

An explorer is a person who combs an area for the purpose of discovery. We did this in North Carolina, Washington, and South Dakota. We may have started with a list but, inevitably, a sign, a magazine, or a person would point us to other places. But I am not the adventurer in the family; Bill is. He is the one who seeks activities or places for excitement or an unusual experience, despite risks. He scuba dives, skis, flies a plane, etc. while I slouch on the couch with my laptop. Lastly, a pilgrim is a person who journeys, especially over a long distance, to some sacred place as an act of devotion. On the way to Minnesota, Bill and I became pilgrims to the Grotto of the Redemption, seventy miles from I-3 and a three-hour diversion from our route. We had seen it featured as the Eighth Wonder of the World in the magazine at Camping World.

It is a complex of nine grottos made from forty-three kinds of gems built entirely by the hands of three men. In 1898, Father Dobberstein, a student of geology in Germany, migrated to the United States to be the pastor in West Bend, Iowa. Almost losing his life because of pneumonia, he built this shrine for the Blessed Virgin's intercession. He used precious rocks he had collected from all over America and from gifts of more rocks from travelers around the world. With Matthew Szerencse's help, work started in 1912. When he died in 1954, it was about 80 percent complete. Rev. L.H. Greving, who had begun to assist him in the parish, continued the work with

Matthew. The Grotto is now estimated to be worth over $2 million in materials, priceless in labor!

Weaving around the Great Lakes States

After the little pilgrimage, we spent three weeks at TT Hidden Bluffs Resort in Spring Grove, Minnesota. It is in a small valley surrounded by bluffs hidden by thick deciduous trees. Our first day trip from this home was to Rochester, 1 ½ hours away. There we passed by the homes of the Mayo brothers and the headquarters of the Mayo Clinic that ranks among the top three in ten of twelve significant medical specializations. Minneapolis-St. Paul, another 1 ½ hours from Rochester, is home to the Mall of the Americas, the biggest mall in the United States, with a theme park, aquarium, entertainment district and five hundred stores. At 4.2 million square feet, it is the thirteenth largest in the world with China in the first two places in the Top Ten and, would you believe, the Philippines in third and fourth!

The next day trip was to the Effigy Mounds National Monument in Harper's Ferry, Iowa, about two hours from our resort. From 500 BC, the Woodland Period Indians regularly constructed the mounds in the shapes of mammals, birds, or reptiles. At one time, there were about ten thousand such mounds. Agriculture has plowed most of them under, but this Monument has 206 mounds and thirty-one effigies, the largest and most fascinating collection, in 2,526 acres.

On the way home, we made another little pilgrimage to the world's smallest church, seating eight people, in Festina, Iowa. We had practically attended mass at a different church each Sunday since we started in June 2009, from the small Quonset huts in the Yukon to the grand cathedrals and basilicas of big cities. But in this little church we began to wonder if we could only deepen our stewardship and establish a ministry if we ended our cruise and joined a parish once again.

As T. S. Eliot said, "We shall not cease from exploration, and the end of all our exploring will be to arrive where we started and know the place for the first time." Around our Minnesota home, we found a sixty-foot waterfall inside Niagara Cave in Harmony and a dozen quilt barns in Caledonia. An Amish buggy was the weekend market in Canton. Rushford Days featured frog jumping and tractor pulling competitions. And we met Alice, the Great Horned Owl, star of the International Owl Festival every March at the Houston Nature Park.

Hiking trails surrounded the resort. One ended with a sweeping scenic overlook of the little valley with the RVs at the campground below. We had fun dividing our time among day trips, hikes, and the hot tub.

In Illinois, our home was TT Pine Country Resort in Belvidere. A refreshing pool

quaint quilt barn

became a refuge during the hot summer days. Downtown is pretty with the few buildings adorned by fifteen murals. Lincoln was stationed in nearby Dixon during the Black Hawk War, and a statue, of a young Lincoln, stands in the town Plaza. But it is Ronald Reagan's Boyhood Home for seventeen years that is the main attraction in the town, together with the world's second largest concrete monolithic statue. At forty-eight feet, American Indian war chief Black Hawk, arms folded, looks far into the distance, towering over the trees on the banks of the Rock River where Reagan worked as a lifeguard.

There are more than three million Filipino-Americans in the country, second only to Chinese-Americans among Asian-Americans. Chicago has the sixth largest Filipino population, behind Los Angeles, San Francisco, Honolulu, New York/Newark, and San Diego. I had two reunions in the city. The first was with some relatives from my mother's town, Rosario. The other was with I/ACT alumni from around the world. After the I/ACT party, Loy, who had made Chicago home, and Fides went downtown with us for deep-dish pizza. We chanced upon many onlookers admiring the glowingly glamorous 36-foot statue of Marilyn Monroe.

From our Minnesota and Illinois campgrounds, we were able to explore Wisconsin even if we did not stay in the state a single night. Right on the Wisconsin–Minnesota border at La Crosse, the World's Largest Six-Pack (giant beer cans) dwarfed the trees and parked cars. From the Illinois border, we toured Decatur Dairy near Monroe, Wisconsin, the Swiss Cheese Capital of the United States and home to the National Historical Cheesemaking Center. Wisconsin supplies 2.6 billion pounds or 26 percent of the cheese consumed by Americans.

The movie Transformers 3 featured the stunning Milwaukee Art Museum, but it was Frank Lloyd Wright who gave Wisconsin a name in architecture. Born in Richland, Wisconsin, Wright built Taliesin East (Taliesin West is in Arizona) a few miles south. It now includes a school for architecture. Another few miles south in Spring Green is the House on the Rock built by Alex Jordan, Jr. from leftover materials of his carpenter father. The Infinity Room juts out 250 feet into the valley that lies 150 feet below, quite a sight from a point down the road.

We were also able to make two little pilgrimages with Fides and Loy. One was to Hubertus where the Basilica of the National Shrine of Mary sits on top of a Holy Hill. A basilica is the highest papal designation given to a building that carries special spiritual, historical, or architectural significance. Inside was a receptacle full of crutches that had been miraculously rendered unnecessary. Then Loy took us further north to Our Lady of Good Help near Green Bay, Wisconsin, just approved in December 2010 as one of only fifteen Marian apparition sites in the world. It was there that a young Belgian immigrant named Adele Brise saw the "Queen of Heavens," dressed in white with a crown of stars, standing between a maple and a hemlock tree.

Adele Brise's grave

Recovering in Indiana and Ohio

Our next home was TT White Oaks RV Resort in Monticello, Indiana. From there we asked Camping World to resolve the heating problem of the RV. We thought the roofing system they had put in Fife before we left for Asia might have messed up the circuit board. Council Bluffs, Iowa replaced the board, but the problem persisted. The branch in Island Lake, Illinois installed a new unit. Rains revealed a little leak, however, and the Greenwood, Indiana branch resolved that. Such is the big advantage of working with a national chain like Camping World.

More than the RV, however, it was Bill who needed the break. His right knee had been bothering him before we went to Asia. We had it checked at The Christ Hospital in Cincinnati, Ohio. Arthroscopic surgery was immediately scheduled. We moved to the TT Indian Lakes Resort in Batesville, Indiana, forty-five minutes west of the hospital, where we stayed for three weeks. After that, we stayed another three weeks at the TT Wilmington Resort, forty-five minutes east of the hospital, in Wilmington, Ohio. That gave him six weeks of recovery time and check-ups at the hospital.

There was a bigger problem though. I had been deathly afraid of fast American roads since the day I arrived in America. I bought a Honda Civic in 2007 and got a driver's license without having to take a road test. I thought that was incredible luck but within three months of getting the license, I was in three separate accidents, without leaving the driveway. I destroyed my son-in-law's garage door, backed into my daughter's Volvo, and bumped into the landscaper's truck! But there was no one else to drive us from the hospital back to the campground after the surgery. Using back roads, it took me 1 ½ hours, double the time, but at least the fastest I had to go was 50 mph. Bill was happy; his knee was healing and an assistant driver was born. He hoped I would continue to drive since driving is a big part of our lifestyle. Thus far, however, I have largely managed to avoid it!

As a matter of fact, to give Bill much needed quiet, soon I left for Las Vegas. I had been missing girls' nights out. My dear friends Jingjing, Ann, and I stayed at the Vdara Hotel. Ann is a tall, elegant lady well-loved in the Philippine computer industry for her skills at organizing, which is why I asked her to join me in I/ACT's marketing group. On the other hand, Jingjing, an experienced and pretty public relations practitioner, had helped me promote many of my successful marketing campaigns and now owns a PR consulting firm. We saw "Thunder from Down Under," Australia's Chippendales (whatever happens in Vegas, stays in Vegas). A Toastmaster friend Angie treated us to a buffet dinner, the "Gordie Brown Show" and the Fremont Street Experience, ending the night at Elvis' White Wedding Chapel. Together with her husband, who is also a nurse, she helped us see that there is more to Vegas than the Strip!

In no time, Bill and I were back on the road to explore Indiana. Nappanee makes 50 percent of the nation's recreational vehicles. We visited the plant of Newmar, makers of high-quality RVs, including our own Mountain Aire. An RV takes months to build and the plant produces about three a week. Models range from 27 to a whopping 65 feet in length. Interestingly, 80 percent of employees were Amish, who don't drive. Project control was surprisingly manual, and the RVs were moved around by pushing them with the aid of flotation pads!

Four major Interstate highways, more than in any other American city, intersect in Indianapolis, Indiana: I-65, I-69, I-70, and I-74. On a Rand McNally map, the city looks like a cobweb. No wonder it has become the Racing Capital of the World. It was quite exciting to visit the Indiana Motor Speedway that draws thousands to the Indy 500. But, since my grandsons were still quite young, I dreamed of bringing them instead to the Children's Museum at the intersection of make-believe streets named Gliceratops and Triceratops Avenues. A huge dinosaur comes out of the wall of a building while another dinosaur's head goes into the top floor of the next!

It was pure luck but we found the home of William Howard Taft, the first Governor-General of the Philippines, right in front of Christ Hospital! He laid the foundation for the country's public institutions and infrastructure. We also visited the airfield the Wright Brothers used, now dubbed the first airport in the world. Bill was most interested in the National Air Force Museum in Dayton that housed 300 American planes used in warfare, including Boxcar, which dropped the bomb on Nagasaki. On the other hand, I was more interested in the Southern and Western Open where I saw my favorite Rafael Nadal in person in my first live ATP tournament! Lest I forget, we also drove to Columbus, the capital of Ohio. The best replica of Santa Maria, the ship that brought Columbus the Explorer to discover America, is anchored there. I could go on forever but I do not have the space to include all that we had seen. We had become more than tourists.

Chapter 14: Taking the Shortest Route to Florida

West Virginia, Kentucky, Tennessee, Alabama, Mississippi, and Georgia, United States
September–November 2011

Gas prices had been rising again, and our motorhome was guzzling gas at seven miles per gallon. We decided to take the shortest route to Florida through Kentucky, Tennessee, and Georgia. That meant we could only take a peek at West Virginia. A camper we met at TT Wilmington Resort had loaned us a DVD of *Mothman Prophecies*, a movie based on strange actual events in Point Pleasant, West Virginia starring Richard Gere and Laura Linney. We took a day trip to this town where the old bridge suddenly collapsed on December 15, 1967, killing forty-six. The Mothman is a large creature with a ten-foot wingspan and red glowing eyes believed to be a harbinger of disaster. He had been seen on the bridge for thirty consecutive days prior to the incident.

From this folkloric little town, we proceeded to the big city of Charleston, West Virginia's capital (population, 350,000). We marveled at the dome of the tallest state capitol in the United States, elegantly crafted with 24-carat gold leaf, from the campus of the University of Charleston across the river. Statues of Stonewall Jackson and Abraham Lincoln guard this magnificent building built after West Virginia was formed out of Confederate Virginia, following a Union victory.

We had not yet experienced any RV mishaps, but as soon as we left Ohio, as we were approaching Louisville, Kentucky, the right front tire of our RV blew out. There were eight tires in all, two in front and six at the rear on two axles. It was such an unfamiliar loud noise and, of course, I got scared. But Bill was able to steer our 20,000-pound rig to the shoulder of I-71. Good Sam arrived within the hour and "unbridled," or freed us, from the predicament.

Loving Kentucky

The original meaning of unbridle is "to remove horse bridles." Horses run unbridled in Kentucky, the "Bluegrass State." The land is good for breeding thoroughbreds that come from three Oriental stallions imported in 1730. I spent many hours looking for bluegrass. After a few days, Bill took pity on me and asked around. He found out that the name comes from blue flower heads that appear when the plant is allowed to grow to its natural height of two to three feet.

In Lexington, Kentucky, the horse capital of the world, we stumbled upon the National Show at the Covered Arena of the Kentucky Horse Park. I think horses are the most beautiful animals and that day the Park had the best-looking of them all. At the Hall of Champions was the living legend Cigar, a leading moneymaker with nineteen wins, sixteen of them consecutive. At the entrance to the Park is the tribute to Man o' War, winner of all but one of his twenty-one starts. He sired sixty-five stakes champions and had the longest stride of 28 feet. On the other side is the tribute to Secretariat,

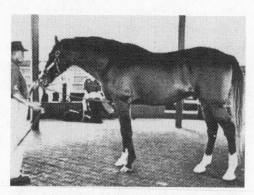

living legend Cigar

the first US Triple Crown champion in twenty-nine years. His heart weighed an incredible 22 pounds, three times larger than the average!

No wonder Churchill Downs, a World Heritage Site and North America's longest operating horse racing track, is in Louisville. Every first weekend of May (the 140th was in 2014) about 120,000 people spill out of the 54,000-seat grandstand onto the grass lawn inside the mile-long dirt track. At this Kentucky Derby, some $150 million are wagered at 3,000 windows. At the back barns, 1,500 future champions are being carefully reared while a serene walkway in front honors those who have passed on.

Men of unbridled spirit also come from Kentucky. I can still hear the thundering applause that always greeted the boxing legend, as he walked into the ring, introduced as "Muhammad Ali...from Louisville,

Kentucky!" Inside the Museum built in his honor, nostalgia reigned as I replayed *"Thrilla in Manila."* Another such man is Abraham Lincoln, sixteenth US President, ranked the best president the Americans ever had in almost all surveys. Fifty-nine steps mark the memorial, one for each of his fifty-nine years, in Hodgenville, south of Louisville. At the top is a replica of the one-room log cabin where he and two other siblings were born.

Kentucky is also home to the Mammoth Cave National Park, which has the longest (394 miles, still counting) underground passageways in the world. Near Rapid City in South Dakota we had also visited two other record-holding caves of the United States. At second-longest with 154 miles (still also counting) is Jewel Cave, named for calcite crystals that produce glowing cave walls. The fourth-longest at 132 miles (also still counting) is Wind Cave, famous for the delicate box work formations and the howling wind blowing in or out depending on barometric pressure.

At our Kentucky home, TT Diamond Caverns Golf and RV Resort, I thoroughly enjoyed the five spa tables and a fully equipped exercise room. One Saturday we went out with friends who had just finished work-camping with one of the Amazon fulfillment centers in the state. They took us to "My Old Kentucky Barn Karaoke" off a dirt road in Park City. *Sans* hat or boots, I believe I was able to entertain the cowboys and cowgirls with my spirited rendition of "Act Naturally."

Driving the Natchez Trace Parkway

In the previous year, we did not have the time to drive the Natchez Trace Parkway and promised we would upon our return. We did! The Parkway commemorates the original route of the "traces" of bison and other game and the earliest Americans on the move. It gently winds from Natchez, Mississippi to Nashville, Tennessee, crossing the northern tip of Alabama.

There were many interesting hiking trails in this forest lane, mostly undeveloped and unspoiled because it became obsolete with the development of river ports on the Mississippi. Fall colors, clear streams, little falls, shallow swamps, gentle meadows, tall trees, and wild turkey were abundant. At Donivan Slough, I was amazed by cotton fields that looked like acres and acres of pock-marked snow.

Then there were the Native American burial mounds, bigger and higher (though not in particular shapes) than the ones we saw in Iowa.

We made two special stops on the Trace. The first was Ivy Green, Helen Keller's home/museum in Tuscumbia, Alabama. Despite being rendered blind and deaf from high fever at the early age of nineteen months, Helen graduated *cum laude* from Radcliffe with the help of her teacher Anne Sullivan. She wrote fourteen books and became a sought-after speaker. She was a major inspiration for my Mother. The other stop was at Tupelo, Mississippi, birthplace of Elvis before he headed for Memphis and stardom. Gospel singing influenced his music so much that they relocated the church he attended as a young teenager to the site of his birth and boyhood home.

Back in Tennessee, one day when I was not feeling well, Bill toured the only Jack Daniels Distillery in the country in Lynchburg. When he got back, he excitedly told me about how Daniels, only seven, started working at the general store owned by the same man who owned the still. When he turned thirteen, Daniels bought it for $25! Years later, going to work early one morning and not able to remember the combination to the safe, he kicked it in frustration, breaking his big toe. Gangrene set in, sadly resulting in his death. Today the company has 400 employees in a town of 500 in a dry county! The United States produces 95 percent of the world's bourbon. The industry has been growing by 20 percent perhaps because of increasing international popularity. In June 2014 we even saw a huge mural advertising it in Brighton, UK.

Putting Georgia on My Mind

When we reached Georgia, Mark Twain's famous quote came to mind: "Travel is fatal to prejudice, bigotry, and narrow-mindedness." Maybe the plantation owners, comfortable in the luxury of their mansions and fields, simply could not see anything wrong with slavery. Georgia was a hotbed, the fifth of eleven states to secede from the Union in January 1861 on the eve of the sure election of Lincoln, an abolitionist, as president. The Civil War that almost dissolved the United States erupted. In 1865 the country joined the ranks of those who had abolished slavery.

From our campground, we took a two-day trip to Atlanta, only two hours away. I wanted to see what a Cyclorama was all about, having missed one in Gettysburg. We found out it was the largest oil painting in the world! Unrolled, it would measure 42 by 358 feet. I thought the admission fee too high but, after viewing the painting and diorama from seats on a huge cylinder that rotated slowly, affording a 360-degree view, I realized it was well worth it.

Just forty-five minutes east of Atlanta is the Stone Mountain. Much like Devil's Tower in Wyoming, it is an igneous intrusion. However, it is more wide than tall, only 1,686 feet at its summit, more than five miles in circumference at the base. It is the largest exposed piece of granite in the world. On its face is the world's biggest bas-relief (three acres, three football fields) of the Confederate pillars: Stonewall Jackson, Robert Lee, and Jefferson Davis.

I thought the Confederate Carving paled in comparison to the grandeur of Mt. Rushmore. It was not proportional to the available area for carving and was not more three-dimensional. Borglum had resigned from this project to work on Rushmore. I repeatedly called it puny. Instead of getting a conversation going, Bill, tired of hearing it over and over, was irked. We didn't talk to each other as we drove around the perimeter road. But the lovely views of the mountain from the golf course across the lake si-

the Confederate Carving

lenced our strife. The view was even better from the grist mill and the 732-bell Carillon off a promontory playing "Ave Maria."

Then I remembered what Oprah once said: "Turn wounds into wisdom." That is what Georgia did, I think, judging by the many great institutions it built out of the ravages of its past. The best example of this past is the Andersonville National Historic Site, a Confederate prisoner-of-war camp that had been filled to four times its capacity. Of the almost 45,000 Union prisoners held there, 13,000 died. It is now a National Cemetery and National Prison War Museum.

The Center for Disease Control and Prevention, created as a US federal agency in 1946, is one of the great institutions in Atlanta. It traced contaminated poliomyelitis vaccine to a California lab in 1955 and tracked the massive influenza epidemic of 1957. An escalation technique eradicated smallpox in 1977. CDC also found causes of Legionnaire's disease and toxic shock syndrome in the late '70s and early '80s. And the AIDS virus was identified in 1981. What a record! The world will forever be grateful. I just hope they can soon find a cure for Ebola virus.

We visited other sources of Atlanta pride including the World of Coca-Cola, the CNN Headquarters, and the Martin Luther King National Historical Site. But the best day trip we took was to Americus, Georgia where Habitat for Humanity has its international headquarters (the US administrative headquarters is in Atlanta). Habitat homes are made using volunteer labor, sold at no profit, and paid for with small monthly payments. I had a fulfilling experience building one Habitat home for the Philippine chapter, together with my staff when I was general manager of MegaLink, the ATM consortium/switch of banks. We even saw the home of Jimmy Carter, thirty-ninth US President, in nearby Plains, Georgia. At eighty-nine, he was still leading, with his wife, a Carter–Habitat project every year.

When we finally reached Florida, we were happy to find that it was not as cold as our first winter there. Ernest Hemingway once said, "It is good to have an end to journey toward, but it is the journey that matters, in the end." We took the shortest route to Florida, but we were still blessed to have seen more than we had ever planned. Cruising is such an enjoyable lifestyle.

Chapter 15: Getting Scared Twice

Florida, United States
November 2011–April 2012

We arrived at TT Three Flags Resort in Wildwood, Florida in time for Thanksgiving. The Resort provided all the roast turkeys, and the campers contributed dressings, sides, and dessert. Bill added a big birthday cake to the spread, so I had an instant party of eighty people! The next day he took me to my birthday dinner at TGIF (Thank God It's Friday) near Universal Studios.

Without any warning, after breakfast on December 8, 2011, Bill felt a terrible pain in his chest; then both his arms started to get heavy. He rested on the couch, but the pain persisted. Then he felt lightheaded and dizzy. Alarmed, he took his blood pressure. It was 166/98 instead of his normal 110/70! We quickly got into the car and proceeded to the Urgent Care facility only a mile from the campground. They told us to hurry to the nearest hospital, the Heart of Florida, fifteen minutes away. Bill drove the car and said, "It is less stressful than watching you try."

At the Emergency Room, he was immediately brought to a bed for tests. By about 1:00 pm the cardiologist-on-call told me Bill had just had a heart attack. My heart sank. They quickly transferred him to the ICU and scheduled a heart catheterization the following morning. That was an invasive procedure! Even if death was rare, in 1/1000 cases there were complications. But he wanted to have it done; not doing anything could have been as deadly. Staff assured me that the hospital was doing about two hundred such procedures a month.

That first night alone at the RV was terrible. As soon as I got in, tears freely fell. He was supposed to be the healthier of us two; I was the one who was having all sorts of issues. He promised to give us at least thirty years; we had just celebrated our third anniversary. We still have a long bucket list; in fact, we'd only just begun! After a small bowl of soup, I reached out to family and friends. Their voices calmed my frayed nerves. I managed to get four hours of sleep.

The next morning it wasn't good to be in the waiting room outside the catheterization lab. The courtesy TV aired a program that was discussing, of all things, the stresses of a funeral. But the procedure was over at noon. He had two blockages, one 100 percent, the other 75. Two stents had been inserted to open the more damaged artery. The other was rescheduled for mid-January to give him rest. The doctor gave me before and after pictures, showing the incredible opening of new blood pathways that were already feeding his weakened heart muscles.

We thanked the Lord for giving us a manageable wake-up call and making it a quick recovery. Bill blamed genetics (his mother and grandmother both had cardiovascular diseases) and his age, about both of which he could do nothing! But he vowed to lose those fifteen unwanted pounds. Prescription drugs would help, but we probably needed to go to Option 4, snow-birding or staying in one place longer, to get more regular and consistent care from a good family doctor.

The day he returned from the hospital, I had sciatica. The excruciating pain forced Bill to take care of me even if he was just recovering. The stress of his heart attack and having to drive to and from the hospital for three days and nights might have taken a toll on me. It became hard to find the spirit of Christmas. We took a vacation from the RV and booked a room at the Sand Pebble Resort, our Vacation Internationale time-share condo in Treasure Island, Florida. It is in one of the thirteen beaches in the region, only two hours from Orlando.

A day after we arrived I woke up with swelling on my left eye. A local ophthalmologist prescribed antibiotics. Then my right eye swelled, and hives broke out in my neck, downward to my arms and torso and, finally, my legs. As instructed, I continued to apply cold compress and cortisone. Otherwise, we were comfortable in our one-bedroom unit, spacious enough for two couples, with a view of the Gulf of Mexico from the balcony. On the ground floor were a hot tub, heated pool, billiards table, and bar. Every afternoon there was bingo, ice cream socials, count the shells, etc. But it was the quiet beach at the back that gave me temporary relief.

The following day we went for a leisurely drive along Gulf Boulevard that connects all the ten barrier islands and thirteen beaches and saw endless rows of beach homes, condo resorts, and palm trees. Just before reaching the Honeymoon Island State Park to the north is Clearwater

Beach. It is famous for its powdery white sand, a beach haven next to a metropolitan area with a population of almost three million, a possible place to settle! I remembered Boracay in the Philippines. Later, we stumbled upon the Mustang Florida Flea Market where we lost each other for an hour to find stocking stuffers for our traditional Christmas Eve gift-giving.

Clearwater Beach

The next day we were drawn to the legendary Ybor City in Greater Tampa. It was the "Cigar Capital of the World" after Don Vicente Martinez-Ybor moved his cigar factory there from Key West in the early 1900s. Other cigar makers followed; then immigrants from Spain, Cuba, and Sicily came to work in their factories. Romanian merchants opened stores while German lithographers brought the latest printing technology needed for the cigar labels. Today it is a lively entertainment and arts district where we saw a demonstration on hand-rolling cigars.

Back in Orlando, my lips swelled again, and weals all over my body became intolerably itchy. We went to an urgent care clinic where a doctor administered steroid shots. But the hives still came back, so Bill's cardiologist referred me to a beautiful Filipina doctor whose tests led her to suspect lupus. She referred me to a rheumatologist who ordered more tests, rejected the diagnosis, and referred me to a dermatologist and an allergist. We still had no clue when we left Florida. The hives would continue to break out every time, it seemed, we came down from the cooler north to the warmer south or there was some pressure on my skin. I changed all my clothes from medium to large.

Getting more anxious about my hyperacidity that had become full-blown GERD or gastro-esophageal reflux disease, I went to the Florida Center for Digestive Health. The doctor ordered an upper body ultrasound and combined endoscopy and colonoscopy. They all turned out to be negative. The doctor said I probably just eat too much or too fast. He was quick to add that I also probably talked too much. Bill could not stop laughing all the way back to the RV, quite loudly!

Getting a Second Scare

In the Philippines, preparations for the Christmas season start as early as the 'ber' months (starting September); America waits until after Thanksgiving. That year I had to wait until after Christmas! Trisha, Claudine, and their families arrived in time for New Years' Eve Dinner at Giordano's near the Maingate Lakeside Hotel where they stayed. The two families spent the next few days enjoying the many treats the Orlando area had to offer: Sea World, Disney's Magic Kingdom, Universal Studios, and shopping at Downtown Disney. Then the couples had their day of rest as we took the four little boys on a visit to Legoland, Orlando's newest attraction designed for kids under nine. They had so much fun they didn't want to leave!

Oh, how we relished those few days with family. Staying connected with the help of technology (Please see Appendix 7, Utilizing Technology on the Go) is a poor substitute to warm hugs and animated face-to-face conversations. Our children live in four spread-out states and three different countries. Visiting each one, giving a more intimate bonding with each child and his/her family, requires more than two months in one round. Reunions take about one or two weeks and give us a better semblance of the whole clan. Clearly, we needed to do both more often.

After the special family time, we headed for TT Peace River in Southwest Florida. I stayed mostly in the RV, watched a lot of TV, poured over tons of magazines, cooked and baked, washed dishes and clothes, did some writing, and kept to myself. I found out that Bill had rediscovered on LinkedIn the college sweetheart he had planned to marry. For five weeks, they had online chats while I languished on the sofa with hives. He suggested that we meet (she had already published a book and might have ideas for me) but I frowned upon the idea. For him, it was an innocent revisiting with a friend he had not talked to for more than forty years. For me, it was outright flirtation. I was shocked; he was frustrated. It was good we had John, our pastoral counselor, who tried his best to help via a few sessions in Skype.

First I was angry; then I was sad. I was already hugely disappointed because we had failed to collaborate on the blog. In the beginning, I had written the posts, and he had taken care of photos. Everything, together with promoting the blog, had become mine. I thought partnerships were working together on a significant joint project. But to Bill it was *my* project, and it had become a chore for him to do what *I* wanted. He felt I didn't listen to his inputs. And then this flirtation! If this had been because I was acting like a teenager and a hopeless romantic, then there was absolutely no more time for me to grow up! It was scary to find out that 75 percent of third marriages end in divorce.

I awakened from my self-imposed exile at a day's caravan arranged by the camp. First stop was Solomon's Castle at the city of Ona about twenty miles away. It is the home and gallery of 72-year-old sculptor Howard Solomon. He built the castle from recycled materials like the exterior's printing plates from the local newspaper. The second was Herrmanns' Royal Lipizzan Stallions in Myakka City, about another twenty miles away. The Royal Lipizzans are the rarest, most aristocratic breed of horses in the world. Born black, they turn into white stallions by the seventh year! The Florida Lippizans had come from those saved

Airs above the Ground

by the father and son Hermanns from the Russian advance in WWII, celebrated in the movie *Miracle of the White Stallions*. They are experts in "Airs above the Ground," leaps and bounds that sow terror in enemy foot soldiers.

My mood remained gloomy, so Bill booked us at the Newport Beachside Resort in Sunny Isles, Florida. We breathed the relaxed lifestyle of South Beach at the southernmost tip of the barrier islands off Miami. Other days we drove through Collins Avenue, its famous high-rise condos, beachfront hotels, and specialty shops and Ocean Drive with its sidewalk cafes filled with people while scantily clad beauties and hunks meandered to the beach. On MacArthur Causeway, we spotted the little islands of Hibiscus, Star, and Jungle, home to Miami's millionaires. Freedom Tower, once the Ellis Island of Cuban immigrants, stood tall at Biscayne Boulevard near the Port of Miami.

On Valentine's Day, we explored Little Havana, the best known neighborhood for Cuban exiles, composed of about twenty thousand households in the blocks around Calle Ocho (SW 8th St.). Bill loved his Cuban espresso and savored the sweet potato pudding at Versailles. At Sentir Cubano, a mural proudly declares Miami as Cuba's seventh province. On a sidewalk in front of Casa Panza, Bill bought three eternal roses from a man who was making them from palm fronds. We loved the atmosphere, canceled our Valentine dinner reservation at the restaurant in our hotel, and perched ourselves at a sidewalk bar table. We loved the evening in Little Havana.

This getaway culminated in a Bahamas cruise, a gift from my three daughters, at the end of which a Slovenian couple we had met in Palawan, Philippines the previous year arrived from Europe. We took them along A1A, the long route to Orlando, and the scenic coastal byway through 350-mile-long beaches. They enjoyed buying hot dogs from roadside kiosks, joined the camp potluck, and loved Walmart's cheap prices! We took them to the Kennedy Space Center's Wildlife Refuge Center in Titusville to see spaceships co-existing with alligators. When they joined other skydivers at Sky Dive City, a 14-acre Drop Zone at the Zephyrhills Municipal Airport, we visited them and later watched them practice at iFly Orlando's vertical wind tunnel.

After they left, we just relaxed at Encore's Lake Magic Resort, even closer to Disney World than TT Orlando. Bill's birthday happily coincided with a street party where we had lots of karaoke singing, dancing, and eating. But during this second winter in Florida, even though it was not cold, we were given two scary wake-up calls: one physical; the other, emotional. We wondered if we should stop cruising and settle down to a more regular life. But did it matter where we were or what we did? Would it soon be necessary to dream and dare again?

PART 3

Becoming Changed

"Like all travelers, I have seen more than I remember and remember more than I have seen."
Benjamin Disraeli

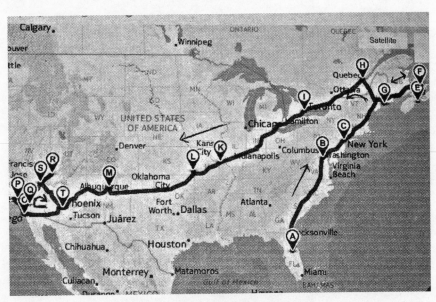

our fourth cross-continent run

Chapter 16: Still Heading North

North Carolina, Virginia, and Pennsylvania, United States
April–May 2012

It was almost a year of cruising, six months on a cross-country run and five months in Florida. We knew we should proceed to Option 4, the snow-birding lifestyle, as soon as we could, but there was a reunion of Bill's close high school friends in Nova Scotia in July. There would be some time to drive up the East Coast and a chance to tour the rest of eastern Canada before going back to Kansas for his 50th HS reunion in September. We were not sure it was the right thing to do, but it was certainly logical, given our goal of ticking off items on our bucket list.

After visiting family and friends in Charleston, South Carolina, we proceeded to the Outer Banks. They are barrier islands that jut out for 200 miles off the coast of North Carolina, 26 miles from the US continental shore. Barely the start of the tourist season, highs of 59°F was made colder by 25 mph winds. This kind of constant wind was what the Wright Brothers lacked in Dayton, Ohio and led them to Kitty Hawk in the Outer Banks. In December 1903, with a bit stronger winds, they flew their plane for 852 feet in about a minute on their fourth try. A memorial now stands on the 90-foot-high Big Kill Devil Hill with the cottages where they engineered the dream down below.

The islands have alluring lighthouses and interesting sand dunes. Ocracoke Lighthouse built in 1823 was still operating. The Bodie Lighthouse completed in 1847 was named after bodies washed ashore from shipwrecks. The Cape Hatteras Lighthouse, known as the American Lighthouse since 1870, is the tallest (160 feet) brick beacon in the world. Finally, there was the Currituck Beach Lighthouse completed in 1875. Despite all these lighthouses, there were many shipwrecks and Ocracoke built a museum called the Graveyard of the Atlantic. Connecting the islands is two-lane Highway 12, separated from the ocean by stretches of sand dunes that seemed to shelter the beach homes. The 426-acre Jockey's Ridge State Park, largest active dune in the East Coast at 30 million tons, moves about one to six feet

sand art in the Outer Banks

southwest each year due to the winds. The Park is ideal for hang gliding, hiking, and kite flying. It was a good thing Bill was able to capture nature's artistry of the shifting sands on our Nikon.

I was thrilled when we came upon the Inn at Rodanthe, setting of the tragic love story, *Nights at Rodanthe*, starring Richard Gere and Diane Lane. But it was soon overtaken by a different feeling when we got to the Lost Colony on Roanoke Island. In 1587, when their leader John White returned from England after asking for more resources, all of the 115 white settlers had disappeared. But braver settlers continued to come. In 1607, Jamestown Colony prospered in Virginia; in 1620, the Plymouth Colony in Massachusetts. They succeeded in planting the seeds of migration. For the next four hundred and more years, an unstoppable influx of dreamers and darers came to America's shores.

Then we moved to the TT Chesapeake Bay Resort in Virginia for *Visita Iglesia*, a tradition of visiting churches during Lent. For Maundy Thursday, it was the Sacred Heart Cathedral in Richmond, only an hour away. On Good Friday, it was the Church of St. Therese in Gloucester, twenty minutes away. For Easter mass, we went to the chapel of the College of William and Mary in Williamsburg, forty-five minutes away. This College educated US Presidents Thomas Jefferson, James Monroe, and John Tyler, US Supreme Court Chief Justice John Marshall, US Speaker of the House Henry Clay, and sixteen signers of the Declaration of Independence. It is the second-oldest higher educational institution in the United States (1693); only Harvard is older (1636). I must add that the Philippines' University of Santo Tomas was established even earlier in 1611.

In Richmond, we discovered a Confederate White House, loaned to Jefferson Davis, Confederate President from 1861 to 1865, during the Civil War. The division between the northern and southern states was that deep! We also found the Hollywood Cemetery, named after the holly bushes that dot the property. Tombs of two US Presidents, James Monroe, John Tyler, Jefferson Davis, twenty-five Confederate generals, and eighteen thousand soldiers, overlook the James River. No other place has that many patriots buried on its grounds. In 1869 a Confederate Memorial was built on the site. The entire area is steeped in history!

Exploring from Greenbelt Park

I was thoroughly enjoying my unintended American education. In fact, the logical thing might have been the right thing to do, especially for the new US citizen. In fact, our next campground, Greenbelt Park in Greenbelt, Maryland, a green space that was part of the National Park Service, was only a mile from the Greenbelt Station of the DC Metro. We were able to tour Washington DC from there.

A trip to the nation's capital is always a political, intellectual, and spiritual exercise. But that time I was visiting the Capitol Building, Supreme Court, White House, and other political institutions as a US citizen. I felt different. I wondered if it was a sign that I was becoming an American, which wasn't bad. But I hoped that I was not forgetting my Filipino roots, which would surely be sad.

The Smithsonian Institute with its nucleus of nineteen museums and nine research centers, the largest complex of its kind in the world, provided the intellectual part. We just had time for the Smithsonian Castle, the headquarters, and the premier museum, the Museum of Natural History. The two face each other and when you look to the right, facing the Castle, you see the Washington Monument; to the left, the Capitol Building. We saw many new exhibits but soon I dropped the intellectual study and dragged Bill to the 45.52-carat Hope Diamond, secretly hoping he would notice that my collection needed a little upgrading!

The spiritual aspect came from the monuments to great men who led the birth and growth of the country. It was eerie visiting Ford's Theatre where Lincoln was gunned down by John Wilkes Booth and the house across the street where he was taken and died. We then walked all the way to the Lincoln Memorial, disappointed, however, that the cherry blossoms were all gone.

The following day, I woke up to another flare-up of hives. I asked Bill to go without me to complete the spiritual aspect of the tour. He visited the Basilica of the National Shrine of the Immaculate Conception, one of the top ten basilicas in the world. He also went to the Washington National Cathedral, sixth-largest in the world and second in the United States. It is the final resting place of Woodrow Wilson, the only US president buried in the capital.

From Greenbelt Park, we were also able to tour Baltimore, Maryland's capital. I learned a lot in Fort McHenry, a star-shaped fort best known for its role in the War of 1812. Nearby towns having fallen, the British Navy had launched a 25-hour continuous bombardment of the city. In the early morning, seeing the American flag still flying from his ship, Francis Scott Key wrote:

"O say can you see, by the dawn's early light?
What so proudly we hailed at the twilight's last gleaming."

Set to the tune of a popular British song by Joseph Stafford Smith, his poem became "The Star-Spangled Banner," America's National Anthem. I thought it was written during the American Revolution. I was wrong! I kept on humming the lines as we toured the 1793 Star-Spangled Banner Flag House, the home of Mary Pickersgill, who sewed the fifteen-star garrison flag that flew over Fort McHenry while the battle raged. The façade of the nearby American Visionary Art Museum also carried the first line of the National Anthem in large multi-colored letters. I found a huge chess set inside with pieces as big as I was. But it was the art car, a glitzy vehicle similar to the jeepney, the Filipino city commuter, which grabbed my attention. I was happy to note that my Filipino sensibilities were still intact!

Discovering Pennsylvania

We had a brief break from our intensive historical tour in Pennsylvania when we camped at TT Hershey Park in Hershey (population: 12,000) popularly called "Chocolatetown, USA, the Sweetest Place on Earth." At Chocolate World, we took the free Chocolate Factory Tour twice! A film about the history of Hershey told about how different types of chocolates tasted, sounded, looked, and smelled. Lots of free samples kept me asking for more at the gift shop that had mountains of chocolate goodies. We looked for the best photo angle of the actual Hershey Factory and its two prominent smokestacks. We found it atop a hill where we also chanced upon the Hershey Hotel, Hershey Garden, Hershey School, and a view of the Hershey Theme Park. At the nearby city of Harrisburg, we were also treated to the nation's most beautiful State Capitol.

Further west, it was good to see that Pittsburgh, the city built from steel that was the foundation of industrial America, had become a city of charm. The resplendent Heinz Chapel was at the center of the campus of the University of Pittsburgh. I was happy to learn that, at the Cathedral of Learning, there will soon be a Philippine Room added to the Nationality Rooms, a collection of twenty-nine classrooms depicting ethnic groups that helped build the city. The city's highest point is Mount Washington. Although two funiculars could take us there, we drove with our little red Saturn instead. At the top, we found "Point of View", a unique statue of Washington and Seneca Chief Guyasuta, finding common ground as they sat, facing each other in 1753. There was also a stunning city view, especially the Three Sisters Bridges, yellow anchored suspension bridges spanning the Allegheny River. Again I was reminded of my precious three daughters.

In Troy Hill, an interesting discovery was Saint Anthony's Chapel, built in 1880 by the pastor, Fr. Suitbert Mollinger, of the Most Holy Name of Jesus Parish. It houses almost five thousand religious relics, the largest collection outside the Vatican, acquired mostly from the priest's money. First-class relics come from the physical body of a saint (or one near sainthood); second-class, possessions of a saint; and third-class, touched by a first or second-class relic.

Two friends joined us in Philadelphia. My dear friend Ann came from her sisters' homes in New Jersey, and Loy, with his fiancée, was on the way to Washington DC from Chicago. Within walking distance from Independence Mall, several landmarks told of America's beginnings. The National Constitution Center is the only museum of its kind in the world. Then there is the President's Site from where Washington governed the nation for two years. The cracked Liberty Bell was just beside Independence Hall, where fifty-five brave men signed the Declaration of Independence in 1776 and

thirty-nine signed the Constitution eleven years later.

In the immediate vicinity of the Mall is Benjamin Franklin's grave at the Christ Church Burial Grounds. Nearby is Carpenters' Hall, built by period craftsmen, where the First Continental Congress, which paved the way for the American Revolution, was held in 1774. Within a short walking distance was the Declaration House where Jefferson wrote the most significant document of the free world, the Declaration of Independence. I stood be-

the Liberty Bell with Independence Hall behind it

fore it in awe, imagining how he got the inspiration for such words as "life, liberty, and the pursuit of happiness!"

The driving tour included sights like the Philadelphia City Hall, at 548 feet the world's second-tallest masonry building. We also stopped at the Philadelphia Art Museum on whose steps the fictional boxer Rocky Balboa trained, and the Eastern State Penitentiary, an American prison until 1971 which emphasized reform instead of punishment. We heard Mass at the National Shrine of St. John Neumann, the first American male saint. Later, we visited the Edgar Allan Poe National Historical Site, one of two homes where he lived (the other one is in New York).

Heading north turned out to be not just the logical but also the right thing to do, at least for me. My intensive though unintended American education inspired this new US citizen. And there would be more of the American story I would learn and America's beauty I would see.

Chapter 17: Appreciating the Northeast

Delaware, New Jersey, New York, Rhode Island, and Connecticut, United States
May–June 2012

We wanted to be in the Northeast in the fall but, because of our schedules, we were there in late spring instead. TT Rondout Valley Resort was our home in the Catskills of upstate New York. It was the home park of friends we had met in Florida, Joe and Dottie. For three weeks, we were neighbors once more. From there, we discovered that the state, crammed into 55,000 square miles, is a dichotomy of rural and urban, traditional and modern, agricultural and industrial.

Joe, a retired captain of the National Guard, took us on a special tour of the US Military Academy at West Point. Standing tall in the parade grounds called the Plains was the statue of the Pacific Fleet Commander of WWII, MacArthur, who returned, as promised, to free our country from Japanese occupation. Fidel Ramos, one of the heroes of the EDSA Revolution of 1986 that overthrew the Marcos dictatorship, was a 1950 graduate of West Point. I answered his call to serve when he was the Philippines' twelfth President. After the West Point Museum, we dined at the West Point Club, overlooking the Hudson, and walked on Trophy Hill where the American Soldier defended his country. A monument called Trophy Point honors him there.

Then we went to the Hudson River Valley, home to many mansions. Lindenwald, the estate of Martin Van Buren, the eighth President, is in Kinderhook. The home and cottages of Franklin Delano Roosevelt, the only four-time elected President of the United States, and his First Lady and UN Ambassador Eleanor Roosevelt are in Hyde Park. Together with the Vanderbilt Mansion, they are all under the care of the National Park Service.

Bill was surprised that I wanted to visit the site of the Woodstock grounds in Bethel, just forty-five miles southwest of our campground. The pivotal music event was the inspiration for my pet project, the Freedom Park, as an elected University Councilor of the Student Council of the University of the Philippines. The 1969 music festival was attended by five hundred thousand and graced by thirty well-known artists such as Jimi Hendrix, Janis Joplin, Blood Sweat and Tears, Credence Clearwater Revival, etc. It extended to nine instead of just three days. The owners of the dairy farm, an alternate site when the city of Woodstock failed to issue a license, have built a simple memorial and a museum of treasured mementos of the flower power period.

We also wanted to go to New York City to live it up. Joe and Dottie let us park our RV at their home in Middletown, New York, forty-five minutes from the campground, with access to the rail service to the city. That gave us the chance to revisit Lower, Middle, and Upper Manhattan one day at a time from the World Center Hotel in Lower Manhattan. Our room looked out at the 9/11 National Memorial. We could see the work going on and the long queue that waited long before it opened at 9 AM. The hundredth floor of One World Trade Center was already finished. When the building was finally completed in 2014, it rose to 1,776 feet, the year Americans declared independence. It is the tallest in the Western Hemisphere and fourth-tallest in the world, a tribute to the ongoing fierce fight against global terrorism.

Just across from the southwest side is the little Catholic Chapel of St Paul built in 1772. An engraved bell on its burial grounds celebrates its miraculous survival from the 9/11 tragedy. Inside is the pew that George Washington used when the nearby Trinity Church, where he regularly went for service, was destroyed by fire. At the burial grounds of Trinity Church rests Alexander Hamilton, first US Secretary of the Treasury and founder of the nation's financial system, whose battle with Jefferson inspired the active ideology-based two-party system. I wondered how we can adopt the same in the Philippines instead of shifting personality-based party coalitions.

Facing Trinity Church is Wall Street. A big statue of George Washington stands in front of the Federal Reserve Building as if watching over every financial transaction. About a block away is the little Bowling Green Park with the Wall Street Bull. Further down the road at Battery Park, we got a glimpse of the Statue of Liberty and Ellis Island, through which all first- and second-wave immigrants had to pass. Both are monuments to what fuels the country's continued progress: innovation coming from new blood that comes to its shores unabated, year after year.

The few times I had been to New York on business, I never found the time to wander around Central Park. Bill and I walked a loop that included the Carousel, the Bethesda Fountain, and the inspiring Literary Walk. All along the Mall were artists, acrobats, jugglers, musicians, magicians, jokers, etc., competing for the public's attention and dollars, performing under beautiful 150-year-old elms. At the end of the loop, we came upon a group singing those old familiar Beatles songs. No wonder, across from them was the John Lennon Memorial, a circular mosaic with the word "IMAGINE" at the center. The Dakota Apartments, where Lennon was gunned down by Mark David Chapman in December 1980 was just a stone's throw away.

On Central Park's southeast side is the Maine Monument just across from the roundabout called Columbus Circle that has a statue of Columbus at the center. Every place in Manhattan is measured in distance from this Circle. Middle Manhattan is where you will also find the Rockefeller Center, the Empire State Building, and St. Patrick's Cathedral. We made it to the 10:15 am Sunday Mass when the choir sang. Representatives of branches of the US military and a few countries were there for Memorial Day celebrations. I felt I belonged.

Besides the subways, the busiest part of Middle Manhattan is Times Square. Bill tirelessly took pictures of me with the Marines, the Army, the Air Force, the Navy, NYPD, and, of course, the Naked Cowboy, who all made the Square extraordinarily festive. At the Times Square Visitor Center, we had our kissing photo taken with the New Year's Eve Ball and discovered a Hopes and Dreams Board on which we posted ours! After a long search, I finally found a $12 top at the American Eagle Outfitters that gave us fifteen seconds of fame on a Times Square screen!

with the Naked Cowboy

Then the time came for us to see *The Lion King* at the Minskoff Theatre on 45th and Broadway in the Theatre District, just beside Times Square. I had been to several Broadway plays in New York before, but this was a spectacle, with incredibly huge colorful props and quite a large singing and dancing cast. After the show, we rode the rickshaw to Ai Fiori (among flowers) on Fifth Avenue. I would never have thought of dining there, but my three daughters gave me a gift certificate so generous it was good for a second dinner the following night! Even though our lunches at Europa Café, TGIF, and Koko's were good, our Ai Fiori dinners were exceptional. The design of the restaurant and waiters' service made us feel we were the only ones there!

In Upper Manhattan, we visited the Cathedral of St. John, the largest handcrafted cathedral in the world. It is an exquisite work of art, inside and out. We also took the time to see the Grant National Monument, one of the top ten mausoleums in the world. Surrounded by stately elms, the edifice features a large marble dome and three levels of marble walls and floors that envelop the tombs of General and Mrs. Grant at the lowest level. Even without air-conditioning in summer, it was quite comfortably cool inside.

The three Manhattans, Upper, Middle, and Lower, gave us everything, the best food, theater, history, events, architecture, churches, memorials, parks, and people. Waking up to a city that never sleeps is a shot of adrenaline for anyone who gets lucky and finds himself in New York City. Can we brave the cold winter and settle there? Nah!

Finding that "Small is Beautiful!"

The country's four smallest states surround New York. Before reaching the big state, we parked our RV at a Walmart in Wilmington, Delaware and toured the second-smallest state in half a day. The Hagley Museum is the site of the original gunpowder factory built in 1802, bedrock of the DuPont wealth. We were more interested, however, in the Old Swedes Church founded in 1638 and Kalmar Nyckel, an old Swedish shipyard on the river, where an old Viking ship was being restored. But it was the 32-foot Shrine of Our Lady of Peace that got our utmost attention, gloriously glowing in the sky. It was made from stainless steel by a Delaware sculptor

After Delaware, we moved on to New Jersey, fourth smallest and most densely populated. The TT Chestnut Lake Campground at Port Republic, New Jersey had just opened the day we arrived so we had our choice of sites. My dear friend Ann, who brought her sisters and brothers-in-law to visit us, saw the lovely view of the lake from the huge picture window of our RV. From this charming home, we went to the southernmost point at Mile 0 of the Garden State (NJ) Parkway in Cape May. Everything was pretty and labeled Cape May, reminding me of a dear friend.

Then we got to the Vegas rival, Atlantic City, playground of the East. To the north is the Absecon Lighthouse, tallest in the state at 172 feet, decommissioned since the bright city lights dimmed its effectiveness. Lucy, a six-story elephant 65-feet-high, 60-feet-long, and 18-feet-wide, made from one million pieces of wood in 1882, is to the south. It is the only surviving example of this novelty architecture. The Atlantic City boardwalk had bright buildings on one side and the charming shore on the other. An Outlet Mall, squeezed into the city streets, had sidewalks with handprints of Miss America winners. I was glad to see

Carol and Lucy

Heather Whitestone's, 1985 deaf Miss America, who did a benefit show for our Philippine Institute for the Deaf.

After New York, we proceeded to New England where the country started. Connecticut is the third-smallest state. Its "Fundamental Orders of Connecticut," is the first written constitution in North America, adopted as early as 1639. New Haven's Roger Sherman profoundly influenced the writing of the US Constitution and the development of the federal government.

Connecticut's geography has given it a strong maritime tradition, but the other important industry is financial services, giving the state the highest per capita income and Human Development Index in the United States. In 1882 when the number of poor immigrants was rising, Father Michael McGivney, currently up for sainthood at the Vatican, founded the Knights of Columbus in the city. It is the largest fraternal service organization in the Catholic Church, with 1.8 million members in fifteen thousand councils worldwide.

Yale University is also in New Haven. Bill had been offered a scholarship to Yale but chose to accept the one offered by Oberlin College near Cleveland, Ohio. Outstanding educational institutions usually spawn excellence in literary works. In Hartford, the capital of Connecticut, we found the Mark Twain House and the Harriet Beecher Stowe Center co-located in one block. *Uncle Tom's Cabin*, Stowe's landmark novel, laid the groundwork for the Civil War. Mark Twain published *Adventures of Huckleberry Finn,* a novel on entrenched racism in the South, just twenty years later.

Rhode Island is the country's smallest state at only 1,500 square miles. It was the first to declare independence from British rule. Roger Williams, the voice of religious freedom and the separation of church and state founded Providence, the capital, after he was forced out of the Massachusetts Bay Colony. His memorial stands on the highest hill overlooking the city at Prospect Park. We lingered until sundown to see Water Fire, an annual spectacle of eighty sparkling bonfires on the city's three rivers with torch-lit vessels going up and down the waters.

We also drove to three picturesque points, Forty Steps, The Breakers, and Ledge Road, of the charming coastal Cliff Walk in Newport. At the International Tennis Hall of Fame where tennis stars get inducted every year, I marveled at the carefully manicured grass courts. After going mad buying souvenirs for the family's own tennis stars, we had lunch *al fresco* on the porch of La Forge beside the Hall, watching cute little colorful cars for two going around town.

Indeed "small is beautiful!" The four smallest states (and the big state of New York) were all charming in spring, with freshness in the air and pockets of delightful little flowers. Beauty in America is everywhere, in all things big and small. It is also timeless; the seasons just give us four versions. We may even try to go when everything would be cloaked in fluffy white snow.

Chapter 18: Getting Moved and Converted

Massachusetts, New Hampshire, Vermont, and Maine, United States
June–July 2012

The rest of New England will also be hard to forget. Camped at TT
Gateway to Cape Cod in Rochester, Massachusetts, we were able
to explore the state, including Cape Cod, known as "The Bare and
Bended Arm in the Sea." It is a vast barrier island with historic
Plymouth at its shoulder. Its upper arm is Hyannis where you can find
the simple Memorial and Museum to honor the beloved President,
John F. Kennedy. I remember crying my heart out as a fifteen-year-old
in Manila when his assassination broke on TV. Harwich, Chatham,
and Brewster counties are its elbow and the Cape Cod National
Seashore, its lower arm. Wellfleet, chosen by Marconi as the site for
his first transatlantic transmission, is its wrist and Provincetown is
its fist.

On a sunny day, we took the one-hour drive to Woods Hole
at the Cape's armpit and rode the 45-minute Steamship Authority
ferry to Martha's Vineyard, the largest island off the East Coast. Its
population of fifteen thousand swells to seventy-five thousand in
the summer. Clustered around the huge tabernacle in the middle
of Oak Bluffs were cute gingerbread cottages in charming candy
colors. A short bus ride took us to Edgartown for a view of the island
of Chappaquiddick, where a female companion of then Sen. Edward
Kennedy (deceased) accidentally drowned.

To the west of our campground was New Bedford, once the center
of the great whaling industry. Its Whaling Museum is still the largest
in the world. At its Harbor, the old Schooner Ernestina was still
docked as a reminder of the whaling days. A Whalers' Memorial
downtown read, "A dead whale or a stove boat" beside the statue of
Lewis Temple, who invented the harpoon tip.

Bringing the Revolution to Life

Because of the well-known Boston traffic, we left our car at Braintree and took the city subway's Red Line. From Park Street Station on Beacon Hill, we chose a Hop-on Hop-off bus service for a tour of the historic sites surrounding the start of the American Revolution. I had read about these at the American School, but this time I would be walking on these time-honored stops. I found myself increasingly moved as we went from one stop to another.

We started at **Stop Nine,** the Boston Tea Party Ship/Museum. In 1773, Boston officials refused to return three shiploads to Britain's East India Company. In the middle of the night, colonists sneaked into the ship and threw the tea into the Harbor. The British Parliament closed Boston's commerce, and a year later the colonists convened the First Continental Congress in Philly. **Stop One** was a close look at Faneuil Hall, a marketplace and meeting hall since 1742. It was the site of stirring speeches by Samuel Adams and others calling for independence from Great Britain. It must have been exciting to live during those times and listen to intensely patriotic speeches. I would have participated, and my Toastmaster's training would have served me well. Paul Revere's house and the Old North Church were at **Stop Two.** A silversmith, Revere rode all night to alert colonial militia in Lexington and Concord, just outside of Boston. Lantern signals from the Old North Church, "one if by land and two if by sea," were to show him how the British forces would be approaching. S**top Three** was the Bunker Hill Monument, where on June 17, 1775 the Battle (fought on Breed's Hill) became the first major conflict between British and patriot forces. The Patriots won! In front of the 221-foot granite obelisk is the statue of Col. William Prescott, who uttered the famous Revolutionary War phrase, "Don't fire until you see the whites of their eyes." The USS Constitution was at **Stop Four** at the Charlestown Navy Shipyard. It is the world's oldest commissioned naval vessel afloat (since 1797). One of the six constructed after the Naval Act of 1794, it is famous for being undefeated during the War of 1812. **Stop Five** was the site of the Boston Massacre where in 1770 a mob had formed around a British sentry, subjecting him to verbal abuse and harassment. Such troops had been stationed to protect crown-appointed colonial officials enforcing unpopular legislation.

Eight other soldiers who came to support him fired into the crowd, killing three. Two others died later. The Old Corner Book Store, Old South Meeting House, and Old State House were at **Stop Six**. We arrived late at **Stop Seven,** the Old Granary Burying Ground, where Paul Revere, Sam Adams, John Hancock, and members of the Franklin family are buried. It was already closed, like the Copp's Hill Burying Ground at **Stop Eight**. That gave us time at Beacon Hill's Boston Commons. Cold beer at "Cheers," of the well-known TV series fame, helped us retrace what we had just seen, the story of America, retold on those nine individual stops!

We also stopped at the Quincy Center station, two stops before Braintree where we had parked our car. The Adams National Historic Site, at the lower-level crypt of the First Unitarian Church, is where John Adams (second President), his son John Quincy Adams (sixth), and their wives are all buried. They were the first father–son tandem in America, followed only by George H.W. and George W. Bush. In Ohio, we had seen the tomb and home of the only grandfather-grandson tandem, William Henry Harrison (ninth) and Benjamin Harrison (twenty-third). The Philippines has only one: the mother Cory Aquino and her son, Noynoy Aquino, the incumbent president.

We had not planned to go to Concord, but Doug, one of Bill's close high school friends, invited us to visit him and his wife, Audrey. He had been a successful financial executive who had lived in London where he founded the European Venture Philanthropy Association. The illustrious city had been the center of two revolutions: the political revolution that led to America's independence and the literary revolution that precipitated the Civil War.

The Minutemen National Historical Park gave me goose pimples. It links the cities of Lexington and Concord. At Lexington, the British infantry force of 700, in search of hidden cannons, easily scuttled the ragtag militia. But in Concord, around 400 minutemen, having been warned by Paul Revere, were ready for battle. The "shot heard round the world" was fired

the shot heard round the world

the next day at North Bridge between the two towns. News spread, and the colonists' ranks swelled to twenty thousand. They hounded the British back to Boston where they won the battle of Bunker Hill!

After American independence had been won, a cultural renaissance began. Concord, with Harvard in Cambridge and the House of Seven Gables in Salem, became seats of excellence in education and literary works in the mid-1800s. The Author's Ridge at Concord's Sleepy Hollow Cemetery is where five great American writers lie together in eternal repose. Ralph Waldo Emerson, Henry David Thoreau, Amos Bronson Alcott, Nathaniel Hawthorne, and Louisa May Alcott all fanned the ideals of individual liberty and equality, leading to the abolitionist sentiment and the Civil War. I couldn't thank Doug enough for giving me this treasured experience

Completing New England

We then took the RV to Camping World in Chichester, several miles northeast of Concord, the capital of New Hampshire. We discovered that four-time Pulitzer Prize winner for poetry Robert Frost's home was just a few miles southeast in Derry. These favorite lines from Frost describe exactly how we feel when we have to move on to other destinations, but pause, before continuing, to catch one last glance at beauty we may never see again:

"The woods are lovely, dark, and deep,
  But I have promises to keep,
  And miles to go before I sleep,
  And miles to go before I sleep."

Eighty percent forest, New Hampshire is gorgeous. I bet it would even be more so in fall. We visited the Silk Farm Wild Life Sanctuary and Audubon Center and the Amoskeag Fishway Learning Center. Then a Scouting Museum we stumbled upon made Bill quite nostalgic. He was a former scout master who guided young men, including his son Jim, to get to the rank of Eagle.

After New Hampshire, we drove our RV to Maine. The state is endowed with a long coastline (3,500 miles), second only to Florida in the Atlantic States. More than sixty lighthouses continue to create drama, cutting imposing figures all along this coastline. The Portland Head Light on Cape Elizabeth is a must-see, the oldest (1791) and most photographed of them all.

Maine beaches are also fascinating. White sands cover much of the southern coast, like other Atlantic beaches, but, as you go north, they become rockier and come with charming coves. Bill took several scenic hikes around Marginal Way at Perkins Cove, very near our campground at

Portland Head Light

TT Moody Beach Resorts. Vacation cottages line Ocean Avenue, hugging the Ogunquit and Wells beaches. At low tide, waiting small boats create plenty of picture-perfect scenes.

I also fell in love with the Maine Lobster, succulent and sweet, especially if done just right. We saw Lobster Rolls being advertised beginning in Massachusetts. At an outlying pier of Kennebunkport, Maine, we had our first, prized claw meat wedged between two slices of bread for $12. The industry is worth more than $300 million a year with six thousand licensed lobstermen in a well-managed sustainable fishery program. I hope we can have the same kind of program for the bountiful resources in Philippine waters!

Maine has diversified from just tourism and fishing. We visited the well-known L.L. Bean, a quality outdoor apparel manufacturer that grew from being a boot maker to a large department store. Shoemart of Henry Sy in the Philippines is very much like that. Celebrating one hundred years, its flagship store in Freeport, Maine has drawn many other retailers, making the town a shopping mecca. We also went to Tom's of Maine, maker of natural organic-based toothpaste, soap, etc. I used it as the case study on niche strategy for my class at Seattle Community College.

When we came back from Nova Scotia, we completed our tour of Maine. We visited Jackson Laboratory in Bar Harbor where, together with twenty-eight other high school students from all over the country, Bill enjoyed a six-week grant from the National Science

Research Foundation. He remembers those times when a large, live lobster cost $1 and burgers, $3! Then we toured Acadia National Park in the eastern part of Mt. Desert Island. "Swimming, only for the hardy," said a notice at Sand Beach. And the hardy frolicked in the ice-cold water! Even if it was low tide, the crashing waves in Thunder Hole still created thunderous roars. We hiked a mile to Otter Cliff, America's highest coastal drop, but dense fog hid what should have been a spectacular scene. The fog even came lower and erased what should have been a postcard photo of Jordan Pond with the North and South Bubbles (hills) at the back. With winds of 29 mph, Bill viewed the entire island from Cadillac Mountain, the highest spot, while I hid in the car!

From Maine, we drove the RV to Camping du Compton in Quebec. It was only two hours from there to Montpelier, Vermont's capital. When the officer at the border asked about the purpose of our visit to the United States, we were not kidding when we replied, "Ice cream!" Four hours of driving just to eat ice cream. After a small lunch at Green Mountain Coffee Café in Montpelier, we drove to the Ben and Jerry ice cream factory in Waterbury. I chose, from among 72 flavors, chocolate therapy, the wickedest chocolate ice cream I have ever had! A magazine at the Café pointed us to the Trapp Family Lodge atop Luci Hill in Stowe where Maria and the Baron recreated their idyllic Austrian life. It also led us to Hope Cemetery, where tombs had sculptures in granite, the primary product of Barre. One had a biplane; another, a soccer ball. Our favorite was the couple lying on twin tombs with the headboard showing them holding hands. Ours will surely be an RV, unless we are cremated. Before driving back to Quebec, Cabot Creamery had a bountiful spread of sample cheese bites for snacks.

Our drive up the East Coast turned out to be the right thing to do. My unintended American education was intensive—an intravenous transfusion, not just an injection. American history came alive, and her beauty jumped out of picture frames. I knew then I had become converted. I was no longer just an American citizen. I had become an American!

Chapter 19: Touring Eastern Canada

Nova Scotia, Prince Edward Island, New Brunswick, Quebec, and Ontario, Canada
July–August 2012

In the following weeks, I was going to be an American tourist in Eastern Canada. The Fourth of July fireworks from a restaurant on the Penobscot River in Bangor, Maine was a fitting celebration of my graduation from an intensive American education. Bill's close high school friend Jim and his wife Carol joined us there, driving all the way from South Carolina where they had chosen to retire. We had visited their Southern home on our way up the East Coast.

The trip to Halifax, Nova Scotia through New Brunswick took seven hours. Other close high school friends of Bill met us at the Immigration Pier, Canada's Ellis Island. We walked with a group to the charming Halifax Public Gardens and the Citadel Fort, sitting atop a hill with a panoramic view of the city. But for Bill, whose roots go back to Scotland, the highlight of our Halifax stay was the Royal International Tattoo Festival, the largest tattoo festival in the world outside of Scotland. Tattoo is the shortened nickname of the Dutch phrase "doe den tap toe," meaning "turn off the tap." It has come to mean the pageantry of power-ful music from marching bands. I found myself heart-ily applauding the large and lively contingent from the United States.

International Tattoo Festival

Then we drove to Antigonish where more of Bill's close high school friends had gathered. One day the entire group trekked to Cape Breton to visit the site where Marconi successfully transmitted the first wireless message between Nova Scotia and England after a storm destroyed the Cape Cod site. After lunch, our sub-group visited the Alexander Graham Bell Museum. Bell was the proponent of teaching the deaf to speak, not to sign, to be better mainstreamed into society. It was the same methodology my mother brought back to the Philippines. On another day, we went with another group to a part of the famed Cabot Trail on the southwestern portion of Cape Breton National Park, all the way up to Cheticamp. It was too bad we didn't have enough time to take on the whole trail, which they say is the loveliest part of Nova Scotia. The week we were there coincided with the Highland Games, and I was lucky to see how they played traditional Scottish games like the hammer throw, caber toss, and vertical stone throw.

The four of us took a short 40-minute ferry ride from Pictou near Antigonish, direct to the capital of Prince Edward Island (PEI), Charlottetown. On the first week of September 1864, Nova Scotia, New Foundland, PEI, Quebec, and Ontario signed the Canadian Confederation at the Province House National Historic Site in the city. It was just like what happened at the Independence Hall in Philadelphia. Canada was born in the east where Europeans had also settled just like the United States, only eighty-eight years later.

From Charlottetown, we moved on to the town of Cavendish, the birthplace of Lucy Maud Montgomery, author of twenty novels and 500 short stories. Her grandparents' property is well preserved, as well as The Haunted Trail and Lovers' Lane written about in her books. The Museum of Green Gables, home of her aunt and uncle where she also spent many nights, had an excellent gift shop. I found a hat with long braided locks, so for a brief moment, I was Anne!

Then I saw why people consider PEI one of the most beautiful provinces of Canada. I will never forget the countryside with bright yellow rapeseed alternating with flowering white and green potato fields. With red and brown houses along the blue river, they created a charming canvass of yellow, green, white, and blue, almost parallel, rows. As if that wasn't enough, all along the coast, we found that the beaches were almost red, coral pink and beige desert sand. Pretty red cliffs surrounded them. We all agreed PEI could very well have been the venue for our reunion.

It was Nova Scotia that was selected, however, due to the tremendous tidal changes around the Bay of Fundy. There were many spots where we could have witnessed the world's highest (up to 50 feet) tidal swings, but Jim chose Amherst, which is also the location of the Fossil Caves Research Center. Beginning at 7:45 pm, each stone or log we used as markers kept disappearing. We saw the tide rise five feet in an hour, a phenomenal show of Mother Nature!

On the road back to Bangor, we stopped at three coastal towns in New Brunswick. St. Martins is the gateway to the Bay of Fundy National Park. At low tide, you can walk to a duo of sea caves and pick from a wealth of enchanting rocks. Next was mostly industrialized St. John, but at the Trinity Royal, the city's 20-block historical heart, the steeple of the old Anglican Church (1789) elegantly rose to 210 feet. Minister's Island, accessible at low tide through a wide gravel bar, is the main attraction of St. Andrew. William Van Horne, an American engineer from Illinois, had been contracted to oversee the construction of the Trans-Canada Railway. He built Covenhagen, a seventeen room mansion on the island. A studio/bath house is perched on a hill, looking out to the sea, leading to the rocky beach below where they had carved a good-sized swimming pool!

Enjoying Quebec and Ontario

From Maine Jim and Carol drove south back home while we crossed into a little bit of France in the province of Quebec, Canada. Street signs were all in French, the official language, with no English counterpart. I had some use for my *un peu Francais*! After the narrow defeat of the Quebec sovereignty movement in the 1995 referendum, Quebec has been officially declared "a nation within a united Canada."

With the Aboriginal peoples also able to preserve their identity in their provinces, Canada has been called a mosaic. America has traditionally been called a melting pot, but growing numbers of minorities have been less willing to be assimilated into a common fabric. When I was teaching "Diversity Issues in Business" in a Seattle community college, a discussion centered on whether America was also becoming a mosaic. There was, after all, an increasing presence of many things Hispanic like TV shows, church services, and others.

The most interesting part of Quebec City is Vieux Quebec (Old

Quebec). A World Heritage Site, it is the only city in North America whose walls still exist. They were built in 1535 (Intramuros, meaning "within walls," in Manila was completed in 1571). The Lower Town consists of the old plaza around the Chapelle du Notre Dame, converted into rows of shops with creative displays. The Old Port was serving the ferries that gave people a view of the city from the St. Lawrence River. You can either walk the steps to go from Lower to Upper Town or like we did, ride on the charming funicular. For a light lunch at Upper Town, we relished authentic *poutine* with all the traditional trimmings while looking out at the dramatic Chateau Frontenac and the statue of Champlain, the city founder. Then it was a short walk to the Basilique du Notre Dame.

Instead of going to the Citadel or the museums, we drove to the Borough de Saint Anne de Beaupre, a suburb of Quebec City twenty minutes away. At the center of town is the Basilique de la Saint Anne de Beaupre with its marvelously crafted exterior façade, exquisite ceiling and altar, and a Cyclorama of the day in Jerusalem when Christ was crucified. On the way back to the city, we stopped at the 275-foot Montmorency Falls, 98 feet higher than Niagara. The paths led us very close to the falls, getting wet in the process. Too bad we didn't have the time to ride the cable car and go up the hill. We would not mind going back to Quebec. It is a piece of Europe in America.

In Montreal our day of sightseeing began just like any other. We went to the Notre Dame Basilica in Vieux Montreal (Old Montreal) with the statue of Jacques Cartier, the city's founder, in front of the square. Surprisingly they charged for admission, so I asked Bill to go by himself while I sat on the steps, admiring the colorful carriages that carry you through the city. Then we had a quick lunch at a nearby Tim Horton's. Just next door, the Information Touristique gave us a plan of attack to take on the Vieux's attractions. Then Bill got the car. As he approached me, standing on the sidewalk, the car stalled, sputtered and stopped.

After he opened the hood and found no clue, he asked me to steer the car as he pushed it to the side of the street. The car was miserably stuck there for nearly an hour, spoiling many tourists' photographs of historic City Hall. Bill tried to cool off with iced tea at a nearby café, waiting for Good Sam. I walked around the block. I found out that all the tourist spots were just around the corner! Bill didn't even have to get the car! It was a case of bad timing.

A Midas truck towed the car (and us) to their branch in Laval, Quebec. Unfortunately, 5:00 pm rolled by and the mechanics still could not find the prob-

the scene in front of Montreal's City Hall

lem. Worse, a power blackout forced the motels in the area to refuse new customers. We could no longer avoid our fate. We treated ourselves to a fine Italian dinner and the comforts of a four-star downtown hotel. The next morning, poorer by a couple of thousand dollars, we got the car back.

We drove back to our campground in Compton to check out. As Bill negotiated the RV around a bend, trying not to hit another RV parked across, he gravitated to a hole where it got stuck. When it rains, it pours! We called Good Sam again, and they sent a big one to the rescue. That afternoon, we finally succeeded in moving on to the province of Ontario.

I had not included Ottawa in our itinerary. I am glad Bill questioned that decision because Ottawa is the government hub that completed for us the four faces of Ontario. It is a bit of England. Every 10:00 am on Parliament Hill, the guards ceremoniously change, like they do at Buckingham Palace. The difference is that Parliament Hill was more photographable. And it was even more so from the back, with a lake below and a view of the Canadian Centre for the Performing Arts above the other hill across the water.

Around Galvin Bay Resort in Lakefield where we camped was Ontario's rural face. Bill ventured on his own and excitedly showed me some of his finds the next day. A house had three huge mosquitoes fashioned out of tree branches and twigs, promoting their tree services. Nearby was the tallest lift lock in the world, lifting boats to about sixty feet. I was not able to see the suspended walking bridge in Cooticook, highest in the world at 150 feet. But in the evening, I also got to see the Lighted Walkway around a Little Niagara in Sherbrook.

Toronto is Canada's biggest city with a population of two million in the city proper and about nine million in the metropolitan area. It is undoubtedly Ontario's urban face. Many spots delighted us: St. Lawrence Market, the CN Tower, an ultramodern City Hall, the Hockey International Hall of Fame, an underground city, and an expo of the 1927 Toronto World Fair. The highlight, however, was our visit with Mon and Marissa, former I/ACT colleagues, who had prospered in the city, both professionally and personally. Mon drove us around in his red BMW convertible, top down, quite an experience for my hair! After a rich buffet brunch at the Gas District and a jolly jazz festival at the beach, we capped the day with high tea at their penthouse. A souvenir photo taken at their balcony had a fantastic view of the Toronto skyline.

Our visit would not be complete without a stop at one of the world's best natural attractions, Niagara Falls, which gives Ontario its tourism face. I had been there fifteen years prior, but it was the first time for Bill. There have been significant improvements on the American side, especially Prospect Point that juts out for a spectacular view of the American and Horseshoe Falls together. Despite this addition, the view is still best on the Canadian side. And at night Niagara is simply mesmerizing. But it was hard to capture its majesty, day or night!

Canada was as exciting in the East as it was in the West. Eastern Canada is replete with the same kind of history as the US East Coast. Come to think of it, the history of the west in both countries is also the same. There are many similarities between the two neighbors. I think such similarities would only increase over time. Canadians are our brothers and sisters in America.

Chapter 20: Going Back to Kansas

Michigan, Illinois, Missouri, Kansas, New Mexico, Arkansas, and Oklahoma, United States
August–October 2012

We wound our way to St. Clair, Michigan from Lakefield, Ontario and camped at TT St. Clair Resort ten miles from the border crossing. It was a day before our fourth anniversary. Bill jokingly said, "With what we have experienced together, we might as well be celebrating our tenth!" I took it as a compliment. That night on the banks of the St. Clair River overlooking Canada on the other side, we had dinner at River Crab and a stroll at pleasant Palmer Park.

Detroit was only 45 minutes from our campground. Clicking "Spirit of Detroit Statue" on our GPS, soon we were in front of a 26-foot bronze sculpture, symbolizing all kinds of human relationships. Across it, at the middle of the street intersection, we were surprised by a 24-foot long right arm with its fist clenched. It was a tribute to former heavyweight champion and Detroit son, Joe Louis. Across the street is the first, and still active, vehicular tunnel in the world that connects Detroit and Windsor, Canada. What a delightful place the click gave us!

We also visited the Motown Historical Museum, which preserves Hitsville USA, the empire Barry Gordy built from the Motown sound he created together with Smoky Robinson, Marvin Gaye, Diana Ross, etc. Going to it was unnerving, as we passed through streets with abandoned dilapidated homes, facades torn off, filled with garbage. There are an estimated twelve thousand such homes in the city that had been declared bankrupt in 2013. The city population has dwindled from two million to less than eight hundred thousand. Although a few areas have been renovated, the scene still reminds one of a pitiful "Paradise Lost."

From Detroit, we proceeded to TT Bear Cave Resort on the other side of Michigan's thumb for another week of rest before moving on to Kansas. We took a day trip to The Presidential Museum and Library of Gerald Ford, 38th US president, in Grand Rapids, Michigan. Bill was a member of the Speakers' Bureau in Seattle during Ford's unsuccessful 1976 campaign. We also took a day trip to the RV Hall of Fame, which we missed when we were in the area the year before. Fifty-five RVs dating from the early 1900s told about the history of luxury camping from the time the wagon was hitched to a horse, a trailer to a Model T, and to today's colossal camping conveniences. There are an estimated thirty million RVers and over eight million RVs.

Our route to Kansas took us through parts of Illinois and Missouri we had not been to before. Springfield, Illinois is Lincoln world. The Presidential Library is in two whole city blocks. It is the most advanced in the world, utilizing all available technologies to make Lincoln come alive. There is a theater where his hologram interacts with other live actors. A wax museum displays his White House stint. Multiple flat panels reenact the crucial campaign of 1860 in present-day newsrooms. At a 4-D theater that told his life story, I involuntarily jumped every time a cannon fired! The National Historic Site, where his home sits, is also on two blocks while his law office occupies another block. Lincoln's remains are in the Springfield Cemetery.

As soon as it loomed on the horizon as we approached St. Louis, Missouri, I couldn't stop taking pictures of the gigantic graceful Gateway Arch. Bill wanted to give me good angles, took a wrong turn and drove us right into the heart of downtown, a no-no land for RVs. Thank goodness

Gateway Arch, with Louis XIV Cathedral

he was able to maneuver us back to the interstate! The Jefferson National Westward Expansion Memorial Museum, dedicated to the doubling in size of the United States after the successful Lewis and

Clark expedition, is a whole complex under the arch. You can take a ride from there, travel inside the arch to its top and exit on the other side of the Museum.

At last we reached Pittsburg for the 50th Reunion of the Pittsburg High School Class of 1962. It was a big success, with 102 attendees, counting significant others. We had the chance to help the Organizing Committee with some of the finishing touches. One of the members was Bill's first girlfriend, Carol, who strikes some resemblance to Elizabeth Taylor. By pure deductive reasoning, I triumphantly claimed that pretty Carols have bookended his life of pretty Judys!

Although I have met many people while cruising, we hardly see them again. Full-time RVing creates enormous distances from family and friends, and most of my long-time ones are back in the Philippines. But in Kansas City Bill's high school friends made me feel like I belonged. So did his college fraternity, Sigma Chi, brothers who invited us to their Octoberfest. I didn't drink a drop, but I felt so comfortable, especially with their spouses many of whom were their school sweethearts. It was like college all over again when giddy laughter ruled.

Amid all the fun, I also got repaired; Jack says, overhauled. I had to have cataract surgery on both eyes. If there is an indication that one is old, it's cataract. But there was still no solution to my hives and GERD. Inconsistent healthcare is the other major disadvantage of the RV cruising lifestyle. It's bad enough that we had both grown older; it is worse that we do not have a regular family physician to help us. Care had been time-constrained and thus palliative. We often joked about how major but easy to diagnose Bill's health issues are and how mine are irritatingly minor but hard to cure.

Because of these two major disadvantages, there may be wisdom in growing roots, even if, as Bill says, we are not trees! Even before we drove up to Canada, this had been an idea whose time had come. We had just postponed it then. It seemed the time for avoiding it had passed.

Making Side Trips from Kansas

Between the consultations and the cataract surgery on my right eye, we drove our little red Saturn to Denver and Boise to visit Suzanne and Jim and their families. When we left Denver for Boise, we spent some time in Salt Lake City, Utah. In 2009 we only had time for Arches National Park. I wanted to see Temple Square, considering a Mormon was running for President. We saw the Tabernacle with the great organ of 11,600+ pipes, golden Gabriel the Archangel blowing his horn atop the Temple, and the statue of Brigham Young, who led the Mormon pioneers west. But there was no sign of Romney.

Between the cataract surgeries on my right and left eyes, we drove to New Mexico. It was the 47th state that entered the Union in 1912, followed closely by Arizona (Alaska and Hawaii came in 1959). Like the Philippines, the two states were discovered by Spanish *conquistadores*. Ferdinand Magellan completed his circumnavigation of the world and settled in Mactan, Cebu in 1521. From Mexico, Francisco de Coronado reached Arizona in 1540 and New Mexico, a year later. Both states were ceded to the United States in 1848 after the Mexican-American War. Fifty years later, after winning the Spanish-American War, the Philippines became a colony.

Immediately upon arrival in Santa Fe, we went to the most famous spots in the city. The Loretto Chapel features the miracle of the helix-shaped spiral staircase that was built in 1872 without using a single nail, reportedly by a carpenter who just appeared, then vanished. Outside, a tree stands, heavy with rosaries from devotees, hanging from every available branch. The Old San Miguel Mission, the oldest church in the United States, dates to before 1628, based on the earliest document found. The best view of the city is from the Cross of the Martyrs atop a hill. It is a tribute to those who perished in the ill-fated 1680 revolt against the Spanish, just like the many revolts Filipinos raised during Spain's 300-year rule of the Islands.

In Los Alamos, northwest of Santa Fe, we completed our tour of the Manhattan Project that changed world history. It was there where a team of scientists assembled the atom bomb from uranium produced in Oak Ridge, Tennessee and plutonium from Hanford, Washington. General Groves took charge of building and maintaining the infrastructure as the scientists pondered upon the imponderables. In July of 1945 the first-ever atomic bomb was tested and detonated at Trinity Site, southwest of Albuquerque. It is open to tourists only two days a year.

We were delighted by the enchanting city of Taos Pueblo north of Santa Fe, a World Heritage Site. It is the oldest continuously inhabited community (population: 4,500) in the country. It lies on ninety-five thousand acres of the Blue Lake Wilderness Area of the Sangre de Cristo Mountains. Red Willow Creek splits the Pueblo into two. The North has the Hlaauma and the South the Hlaukkwima, two Great Houses more than one thousand years old.

enchanting Taos Pueblo

American Indians were said to have come to America thirteen thousand years ago, by land bridges or coastal boating. Then they spread out across North America which became a patchwork of differing cultures, dialects, and societies. Later there was a flourishing of Native-American culture. There are 150 Great Houses on a 180-mile road network first noticed in the 1900s and still expanding with new discoveries. Chaco Culture National Historic Park, about 150 miles west of Santa Fe, best exemplifies this period.

Chaco must have been the center of learning, trade, and worship around 900 to 1115 AD. It stretches ten miles into the San Juan Basin; made up of the ruins of nine Great Houses connected to one another by roads. Each Great House had one or more underground chambers called *kivas*. The material used was sandstone. Log sections were also used to reinforce the structure tightly to become multistory. The rooms were arranged in grids connected by doorways and vents. The most thoroughly studied, largest, and best-preserved was Pueblo Bonito with 650 rooms.

We completed our tour of New Mexico with a short visit to Albuquerque. The Petroglyph National Monument reveals as many as twenty thousand American Indian petroglyphs in rocks along two paths. We also tried the Sandia Peak Tramway, the third-longest (7,720 feet) clear tramway in the world. Finally, we shopped for colorful southwestern craft at Old Albuquerque.

Back in Pittsburg, while waiting for the healing of my eyes, we visited a few other places we missed the last time we were there. We went back to Kansas City to see the Public Library, designed with the spines of thirty-two of the best-loved books of all time for its façade. Books stacked on top of one another are the entrance steps. In Independence, Missouri we visited the home, gravesite, and library of the thirty-third President, Harry Truman, who made the most difficult decision of ordering the dropping of the atomic bomb.

We also took the RV to Jay, Oklahoma, just two hours from the Docks for a week to explore more of Arkansas. Walmart's first store and headquarters are in Bentonville. The 67-foot Christ of the Ozarks, the fourth-largest statue of Christ in the world and the largest in the United States, is on Magnetic Mountain. Nearby, the biggest tuned wind chime in the world, the Celestial Wind Chime, hangs 36 feet from a tree. Finally, we found the small charming stone home of Bill and Hillary Clinton near the University of Arkansas in Fayetteville where they had been professors.

In Oklahoma City, the center of forty-three American-Indian tribes, we saw the grand memorial built for the victims of the bombing of the Alfred P. Murrah Federal Building. It had been the largest terrorist attack before 9/11. Two pillars marked 9:01 and 9:03 are at each end, with shimmering shallow water between them and 168 empty chairs at the side.

But we could no longer postpone our decision to proceed with Option 4. We decided it was time to look for a base and snow-bird in the winter of 2013-2014. Bill noted we were younger than many we had met in campgrounds and feared stress might be greater if we settled into just one place, especially with my propensity for boredom. But we also knew there are different notions of fun (Please see Appendix 8, My Different Notions of Fun). Snow-birding would just be a chance to experience other shapes and sizes of it.

Chapter 21: Looking for a Base

Arizona and California, United States
November–December 2012

In a sense, we had been traveling the country to find where we belonged and where we can later settle. Florida, Arizona, and California, with climates reasonably close to what I am used to, emerged as candidates. Proximity to our children's homes eliminated Florida. And, while taxes in California are higher than Arizona, we wanted to see if any advantages would trump that.

As we entered Arizona from New Mexico, right after the large Navajo truck stop, we discovered that the Petrified Forest National Park and the Painted Dessert saddle both sides of I-40. One can view fifty thousand acres of petrified wood from trees that grew there about 225 million years ago from the 28-mile park road. Blue Mesa and the Teepees are stunning vistas. Too bad we reached the Painted Desert at sundown; our camera just could not capture the amazing canvass.

Soon we reached our first possible base in North Central Arizona, TT Verde Valley RV Resort in the lower valley of Cottonwood (population: 11,000). Just minutes from the resort are two spots named after Montezuma even if he was never in the area. Montezuma Castle is one, an elaborate five-story 100-room dwelling built around 1100 AD into the soft limestone cliff standing 100 feet above the valley. The other is Montezuma Well, a natural sinkhole with fifteen million gallons of water; baffling many as to how it is replenished from the surrounding dry area. About ten minutes away the Tuzigoot National Monument, built between 1125 and 1400 AD, crowns the summit of a long ridge rising 120 feet above the valley floor. Up in the hills, only twenty minutes away, is the old mining town of Jerome from where the view of the valley was simply stunning. I was happy to find a Filipino and his partner who owned a curio shop up there.

Even Sedona (population: 10,000) is a mere thirty minutes northwest from this base. Imagine a city within what should be a national park. Outstanding red rock formations named after their shapes, such as Cathedral, Bell, and Coffee Pot Rocks, etc. are all around. Real estate must cost a fortune there! The Chapel of the Holy Cross soars ninety feet into the air on a thousand-foot high rock wall. It offers spectacular views and a serene spiritual retreat. At sundown, we were rewarded with an outstanding view of the city and the rocks from the Airport Overlook.

Going further north took us to Flagstaff (population: 60,000), less than an hour from Cottonwood. Its Old Historic District has the Giant Pine Cone hanging from a roof that, like its counterpart glittering ball in New York, falls at the countdown for New Year! The city also boasts of three national monuments. The Sun Crater Volcano National Monument features the thousand-foot high cinder cone volcano. Then there is the thirty-five thousand acres of the Wupatki (meaning tall house) National Monument where ruins of twenty-nine structures remain. Lastly, the cliff dwellings of the *Sinaguas* (meaning, without water) comprise the Walnut Canyon National Monument, carved into the natural recesses of the canyon, about three meters deep.

The most stunning of them all is the Grand Canyon National Park. The East Rim, where a watchtower offers Desert View, is only two and a half hours from Cottonwood. Going west on Canyon Rim Road, we reached the South Rim in just thirty minutes, stopping at every overlook, each pro-viding yet another majestic view. At South View, I had another photo of my life taken at Mather Point. As the crow flies, the North Rim and the South Rim are just ten miles apart but the entire rim is 215 miles long. I had joined a small plane flight over the Canyon with

Mather Point, Grand Canyon

my daughter April years before, but this drive with Bill gave me much closer and more impressive views.

Though North Central Arizona is truly spectacular, Cottonwood, Sedona, or Flagstaff will not make the finals in our selection of places to settle, however. It was just November, and it was already a little cooler than we would like our base to be. Just imagine what it would be in the dead of winter! Besides, I am a big-city girl.

Looking at Bigger Cities

From everything we heard: city size, temperatures during winter months, and other factors, Tucson was getting to be at the top of our list. Excited, we went to inspect six City RV Resorts and chose the Voyager RV Resort, with 1,500 sites, full amenities, a host of clubs, and even a motel for visitors, a finalist. Tucson (population: half a million, metropolitan area: one million) already has Hispanic whites as the majority, which is what the whole country will look like in 2050. At sundown, we drove to the Sentinel Peak for a good aerial view of the city.

University of Arizona (UA) is in Tucson and owns the only Biosphere 2 in the planet, designed to mimic Biosphere 1 (the earth). It was an incredible venture started in the late 1980s by Texan billionaire Edward Bass who put in $250 million to create five different ecological systems: tropical rainforest, savannah, marshland, ocean, and desert. In the early 1990s, eight Biospherians (four women and four men) lived there for two years. The University has since added a Landscape Evolution Observatory to study water conservation.

Spanish influence is all over Tucson. Founded in 1692, the Mission San Javier del Bac is the finest example of Spanish colonial architecture in the United States. We attended Mass on St. Francis' Feast Day, December 2. There were ground fireworks, and we had good eats from kiosks. Another church south of Tucson is the lovely Tucumcacori Mission built in 1691 where Juan Bautista Anza, a Basque Spanish explorer, started the trail of missions to California.

On the way to our campground, we drove through the two sections of the Saguaro National Park where the saguaro cactus, which can grow up to seventy-five feet, thrives. What we liked most about our camp, the St. David RV Resort, are the nearby towns. Tombstone, a former silver-mining boomtown, was the site of the 1811 Gunfight at O.K. Corral. About an hour south sits Tubac, where we enjoyed December's *Iluminaria* Nights when thousands of lights adorn sidewalks and stores. At a restaurant there, we discovered *molcajete*. It is beef stewed with cactus in a volcanic pot that kept the dish simmering till the end of dinner. Up the hills near the Mexican border is Bisbee, the setting of many of the mysteries of best-selling author J.A. Jance.

On the other hand, Phoenix is the fifth-largest city in the country with a population of 1.6 million, following New York City, LA, Chicago, and Houston. The population in the metropolitan area is around 2.5 million, same size as Seattle and Denver. Because of relatively warm sunny winters, its suburbs abound with many retirement communities and huge City RV Resorts like the Viewpoint RV and Golf Resort with 1,900 sites. It has two clubhouses, two golf courses, ten tennis courts, six pickle ball courts, and a ball park. There are three swimming pools, six hot tubs/spas, a large fitness center and a sauna. Billiards, card, wood carving, jewelry making, computer and other rooms are available. There are a library, bar and grille, salon and spa and pro shop. You can also choose from fifty clubs such as book, poker, bridge, photography, tai chi, yoga, writing, dancing, karaoke, billiards, hiking, etc.

I was pleasantly surprised to find that Phoenix is a pretty city, too. It is a desert green with swaying palms, small and huge cacti, and lots of *palo verde* trees that burst with tiny yellow blossoms in spring! The Desert Botanical Garden displays unusual greenery that has adapted to an otherwise arid land. There is a stunning city aerial view from Dobbins' Lookout on South Mountain and Superstition Mountain on the Apache Trail lords it over many RV Resorts. From the Hole in the Rock nearby, it was nice to look across Papago Park to the glistening pyramid atop another rock, the tomb of Hunt, the first state governor who served seven terms.

There is remarkable architecture in the city, too. We have long wanted to tour Tovrea Castle that looks like a huge wedding cake, but the waiting line for tours is always six months long. The Mystery Castle is a Dad's interpretation of his daughter's fantasy while the Wrigley Mansion is the legacy of the chewing gum magnate. Taliesin West is the companion masterpiece of Frank Lloyd Wright's Taliesin East in Wisconsin. And right in the middle of Phoenix is Pueblo Grande, the Hohokam Ruins that thrived from 900 BC to 1450 AD.

I am partial to bigger cities, so we decided to proceed to San Diego to complete our research. We canceled our trip to Lake Havasu and Bullhead City in northwestern Arizona. But since Yuma was on the way, we checked it out and spent Christmas there. Its population of one hundred thousand doubles at winter time. The Valley is a charming agricultural area with acres upon acres of whitish cauliflower, green lettuce, and purple and green cabbages. There are many City RV Resorts, but we did not find any as big as Voyager or Viewpoint.

Yuma is only eight miles from Mexico. After leaving our car in a parking lot, we easily walked into the town of Los Algodones just across the border. The whole town consists of four blocks of dental, optical, and medical clinics, as well as pharmacies and other stores that allow Americans (and Canadians) to fill their needs for a song. I should have done my overhauling there! Vendors of Mexican goods that are "almost free" line the sidewalks. You have to be a good negotiator though. Aside from shopping for inexpensive products and services, we also feasted on authentic Mexican food and partied at Paraiso. Mariachis were playing "cowboy" and Mexican songs that got us dancing rock and roll, cha-cha, and everything in between.

And yet, I do not see myself being happy in Yuma for long. It is too small a metropolis for a big-city girl like me. As weeks roll by, new options for fun would get fewer. In fact, we reserved for two weeks, but we cut our stay to just five days, with a day in Mexico to boot. Besides, Los Algodones is quite accessible from either Tucson or Phoenix.

We arrived at TT Pio Pico Preserve in Jamul, California, east of San Diego, just in time for the campground-hosted New Year's Eve Party. I was terribly disappointed, however, to find out that City RV Resorts were more like family weekend vacation places, meaning there are many kids running around, with less than three hundred sites. We found only two that were bigger: Campland on the Bay in San Diego had six hundred tiny spaces. The one in Hemet had 1,100, but it was one-and-a-half hours away from either Los Angeles or San Diego.

Still, we enjoyed San Diego's highlights. The Cabrillo Monument at Point Loma is a great place for an aerial view of the city. On the way to Point Loma is the Navy Memorial Park where the gravesites seem to mesh meaningfully with the sea. Old Town San Diego was colorful, but their *molcajete* was not as good as

Navy Memorial Park

the one in Tubac. We had a hard time looking for the Military Salute to Bob Hope but finally found it on a mound beside where the USS Midway was anchored. His monologs played continuously to an audience of sixteen bronze statues.

A Filipino community is a definite plus for San Diego, however. One night, at a Fil-Cuisine restaurant, a Caucasian male was challenged by a group of lovely Filipinas to try a delicacy called *balut* (boiled duck egg with a young embryo inside). He said he would if Bill joined him. Mr. Adventurer agreed. That was the first, and probably last, *balut* ever for the two gentlemen! My dear friend Jingjing also told me to check out the Surf and Turf RV Park located close to the beach and at the State Fairgrounds in Del Mar where a lot happens year-round. It was managed by her good friend but, unfortunately, the campground was too small. But on New Year's Day we all had a Filipino lunch together at the home of a Filipino family Jingjing was visiting. We even had a Filipino dinner that night with another family, friends of her friend. Such is Filipino camaraderie. It will fill your tummies with great food and your spirit with spontaneous laughter.

Even if a Filipino support system would be available to me in San Diego, taxes are just way too high, evident in the high cost of living in California. It was beginning to look like it will be between Tucson and Phoenix in Arizona. Bill thought we had best postpone our decision. We decided to make a reservation only after the road trip to Seattle and a reunion with my family.

Chapter 22: Completing the Trail

California, Washington, Colorado, Kansas, Utah, Nevada, United States
January–May 2013

After resting a few days in TT Soledad Canyon RV Resort in Acton, California, we packed for our two-month break, stored the RV, and drove to Seattle. For the sake of family, we were doing what RVers are not supposed to do. We were driving *to* a cold place instead of *from* one! But it was fascinating to see the scenes change—from brown mountains and green fields to mountains of white and leafless trees, then to snowy mountains with patches of evergreens.

We arrived in Seattle on a late January night. Dinners with friends and family, visits to the doctor, LA Fitness workouts, and Seattle Seahawks' games filled the next days. Bill bravely had his hair cut by my granddaughter Krishna at Gene Juarez Beauty Academy. She would be graduating in a month, having survived through a student loan and a patchwork of jobs.

On the fifth day, Bill left for Boise for a whole month. He went to help spruce up some space for Jim's law office in the building he and his partner had acquired. It was going to be the longest separation in our four years of marriage. At first Bill didn't believe in time apart but, in a complete turnaround, he said he began to consider this while we were looking for a base.

In Mark Twain's *Innocents Abroad*, Tom Sawyer said, "I have found out that there ain't no surer way to find out whether you like people or hate them than to travel with them." Did we make a mistake by not proceeding with Option 4 as early as possible? John directed each of us, every single day we would be apart, to find meaning in a memorable adventure and to reflect on how it was to be with the other. We also had to read *Perfect Love, Imperfect Relationships*.

The first days without him were hard. I tried to read the book assignment. My reflections led me to a review of all the posts in my blog. I saw our story developing behind the scenes. In Option 2, we were distracted by the fast pace of sightseeing but in Option 3, we began to have more days of ordinary married life. As Elizabeth Gilbert warned, "traveling-to-a-place energy and living-in-a-place energy are two fundamentally different energies." We did not notice that a room for disappointment opened wide when spectacular scenes were no longer often readily at hand. I compiled all the posts into one manuscript. Lo and behold, I had my first draft of a book! Sad moments always move me to turn elsewhere with redirected passion.

On Valentine's Day Bill was at the door with a huge vase of exquisite yellow flowers! That night we went out for paella at La Flora, a Spanish restaurant. With what I would now call a stroke of masterful luck, my doctor had changed my medications that day and a new, much calmer Carol emerged. Bill thought the hands of time were turned back to when we first met. Even the Oscar movie marathon at Regal Cinemas—nine nominees for Best Picture in the 2013 Oscars shown for two days at only $50—helped. Everything conspired to help us be together again.

We had serious talks, some by ourselves, others with John. Bill confessed that he and his former college sweetheart chatted several times over the phone during his month away. That hurt me a great deal, but I thought it best to be his friend first. I listened to him more. He said, "I found out how much we had both changed. We no longer had much in common. My inquisitiveness is over. How I wish you had accepted it right away for what it was, simple curiosity." The openness led us to share our difficulties, the rigors of the road and our health issues. I particularly decried the lack of support system, essential for the Filipino. Bill, who had waited to do meaningful payback activities upon retirement, longed to start one. My writing, preoccupation with social media, and fun at online word games had made him one very lonely computer widower.

How bad could the odds have been for this "young" marriage? We did not know our limitations when we started. Our life habits, good and bad, were in full color. There was nowhere to hide. There was no truth to the quote we found on a throw pillow at the Palm Springs Villagefest, "We get along in our RV 'cuz we have no room to disagree!" All couples disagree, about things, big and small. As a matter of fact, when people find out that we had been RVing full-time for so many years, they congratulate us for having been able to remain friends.

We had a few pluses. We shared the love of travel and respected each other for what we had each accomplished before we met. We had extended our honeymoon for as long as we could, knew when we needed help, and sought it. At least one of us knew more about being a partner, and that wasn't me! I realized I had to grow up, learn that not every encounter with the opposite sex is flirtation and accept that partnership is not about working on the same *one* thing. In a different sense, I had completed another trail; I had finally become a wife! Together we made reservations to snow-bird for six months at Viewpoint in Mesa, Arizona starting October 2013.

Resuming the Cruise

After a successful reunion with the whole family that was finally complete again after Mexico (April, working in England, did not make it to Orlando), we drove back to California. Everything had started to burst into brighter greens and yellows. It was another

spell-binding shift of the seasons. From Acton we proceeded to our favorite TT Palm Springs Resort. We felt warm, so warm that my hives flared up again! Come to think of it, my hives first appeared when we arrived in Florida. I may no longer be used to the kind of weather that I lived in for fifty-four years. I hoped not, or Phoenix would be a disaster!

It was a thrill to be in Palm Springs again that winter. "Marilyn Monroe"

under Marilyn Monroe's spell had moved from Chicago,

Illinois, where we first saw her, to downtown Palm Springs on the corner of Tahquitz Canyon Way and Palm Canyon Drive. The 36-foot statue is moved to a different location every year. Bill finally had his dream photo taken under her skirt and spell! At the famous Plaza Theater, the Fabulous Palm Springs Follies featured a unique cast: the oldest male performer at eighty-four and the female, seventy-seven! Too bad the show ended in 2014. I could have had a new career! Leslie Gore (now deceased) was the main show, however. She wowed the audience with her hit songs, "It's My Party," "Judy's Turn to Cry" and "You Don't Own Me."

After April Fools' Day, we left Palm Springs for the wedding of Bill's niece in Kansas. We stored the RV at St. George KOA campground in Hurricane, Utah and drove to Suzanne's in Denver, moving from white sands to red hills to snowy mountains. The visit was short and in the last two days it snowed a lot. We were forced to drop our plan of going northeast to Nebraska to see Chimney Rock and catch the migration of 80 percent of the world's sand-hill cranes.

Instead, we chose a southern, warmer, more direct route on I-70 through Wichita, Kansas. On the way, we saw many scrub oaks that glistened from the freezing rain, turning leafless branches into a delicate ice sculpture. Unfortunately, the Nikon could not seem to capture the sparkle of the trees. We visited the Dwight Eisenhower Presidential Library and Museum and boyhood home in Abilene. As Supreme Commander of the Allied Forces in Europe, Eisenhower strategized the defeat of the Nazis through the largest military deployment on D-Day, June 6, 1944, at France's Normandy Beach. After this, he was ushered into a two-term presidency in peacetime prosperity.

We arrived in Pittsburg the day before the wedding reception and the next day we were on our way back. We stopped for the night at Dodge City where the Longhorn steer and Wyatt Earp statues lord over downtown. The town, Cowboy Capital of the World, features the Cattle Feed Lot Overlook and the wagon wheel ruts at the Santa Fe Rail Tracks. We also stopped in Oakley, birthplace of Buffalo Bill.

After another snowy visit at Suzanne's in Denver, we stayed for a night in Utah. In 2009 we took a peek at Arches National Park and visited Salt Lake City three years later. This time we toured Arches' companion Park, Canyonlands. It has four districts: the Island in the Sky, the Needles, the Maze, and Horseshoe Canyon. When we got back to the St. George KOA campground, we took the time to visit

Zion and Bryce Canyon National Parks. Zion, meaning sanctuary, is a surprising spectacle of soaring cliffs surrounding a deep canyon. But the Bryce Hoodoos, intricate formations still being crafted by erosion, seemed like delicate cities for extraterrestrials. Wide pockets of them were on the 37-mile drive in the Park, at seven thousand feet.

hoodoos in Bryce

Soon we reached Nevada for our month in TT Las Vegas Resort. Crowds were there, even if it was off peak in a sluggish economy. Like us, many did not come to the casinos but for the shows. You can find many that are free if you just know where to go. Tony, a friend and former Country Manager of IBM Philippines when I was a young marketing representative of the firm, had retired in the city and showed us a few. The Pinoy Pride Celebration included the traditional *Santacruzan* (a religious procession of beautiful maidens) and the Jabbawockeez, a multicultural group founded by Filipinos who won America's Best Dance Crew, now a Luxor mainstay. Tony also told us to go to Fremont for the Elvis Contest that sought the representative to the Memphis National Search. I enjoyed that a lot and had photos with five Elvises!

Circus Circus, Mirage, Treasure Island, Bellagio, and Caesar's Palace are familiar places. But the "Lake of Dreams" in Wynn was our best find. It is a mechanized fairy tale with thirty-foot-wide flowers that sway. Seven projectors give life to a thirty-foot-tall head that rises from underneath the lake, singing, talking, and making faces at the audience. Luckily, a guard showed us a secret balcony on the second floor where we watched part of the show without having to dine there.

The shows that were not free were even better. On Mother's Day, Angie and her husband treated us to the longest running show of drag queens on the Strip, "Divas Las Vegas." Three days later, they brought us to Planet Hollywood's "Really Hypnosis, Really Funny" by Marshal Sylver where the most easily influenced volunteers became the show. Claudine had also gifted us with tickets to "Jersey Boys," the longest running musical in Vegas. On Mother's Day, Bill took me to "Tournament of the Kings" at Excalibur Hotel. At the Round Table banquet, we ate a whole Cornish hen with our fingers and drank from our tankards, which we raised, shouting with all our might "Huzzah" for our King to win. Despite a brave fighting stance, we lost!

We were also happy to find that five nature breaks were close to the Strip. Red Rocks Canyon National Conservation Area was only thirty minutes away, providing views of desert beauties. Forty minutes away was Mount Charleston, a haven in summer for temperatures cooler by twenty degrees, much like Tagaytay is to Manila but a lot closer. Hoover Dam, a concrete arch-gravity dam, was only fifty minutes south of Las Vegas together with Lake Mead, the first National Recreation Area created during the dam's construction. Valley of Fire was only fifty miles northeast of the city. Its name comes from red sandstone that appears to be on fire when hit by the sun's rays. Even Death Valley National Park was only two hours away. It is the driest place in America, averaging two inches of rainfall a year. It is also the eighth lowest place at -282 feet and holds the eighth hottest (134° F) recorded temperature in the world.

Although nonstop entertainment and Filipino friends were pluses for Las Vegas, we did not change our mind about Phoenix. It ranks fifth-best in healthcare in the country and temperatures are warmer by ten degrees during winter. Besides, Las Vegas is only five hours from Phoenix.

After four years of driving on good and bad roads, we finally made it; we completed the trail. In another sense, I also completed another kind of trail, the journey of finding true love. I had traveled and loved, not just a little, but a lot. And I was glad I dreamed and dared.

For those who would like to join the 1.3 million full-time RVers, please see Appendix 9, the "Ten Commandments of Full-time RV Cruising." Most of the lessons are suitable for any lifestyle. After all, cruising is not about a mode of transportation. It is about a pace of travel!

Conclusion

Completing the Dream

"The real voyage of discovery consists not in seeking new landscapes, but in having new eyes."
Marcel Proust

Alberta, Canada and Washington, Colorado, Arizona and California, United States
June–October 2013

In late June 2013 we stored the RV in Cottonwood, Arizona to go to Calgary, Alberta for the birth of my fifth grandchild and the famous Calgary Stampede. While we were there, our little red 1998 Saturn, with more than two hundred thousand miles, suddenly died! Luckily we found another Saturn, a tan 2002 that even matched our motorhome.

To catch our fifth-anniversary date at the Visa Signature Event in Madison Park Conservatory in Seattle, Bill drove for twelve hours straight. After just two days in Seattle, he put in another nineteen hours in two days to catch his Denver grandkids' last weekend before school. While in Denver, his left knee suddenly hurt badly. At the hospital, we found out that blood clots had formed. It was a case of deep vein thrombosis. The doctor let us resume our road trip only when his International Normalized Ratio (INR) returned to 2.0. It was another lesson we still needed to learn. Everything must be in moderation.

Back in Cottonwood, I was greeted with another bout of hives. Good thing my dear friend Ann visited and introduced me to her sister who lived in the area. She would be a familiar Filipino face I could count on when necessary. We chilled out, and my hives subsided. But only about a quarter of an hour after we left town, our rear tires blew out! We got towed to a repair shop in Phoenix near midnight. The tires had not only exploded, but the flying tire bits had also damaged the drive shaft. The RV had to have a lot of repairs, including overdue body work.

While all the repairs were being done, we visited Krishna, who was already working at the plush Salon Nesou in Santa Monica. That gave me the chance to go to the Philippine Consular Office in LA where I could apply for dual citizenship. I had to renounce my Filipino citizenship when I took my oath as a US citizen. I was sad that, in being one, I technically ceased to be a Filipino.

The difference between a US permanent resident and a naturalized citizen is that the latter can vote (or run for an elected post office). I cast my vote for the very first time via guaranteed express mail delivery in the 2012 presidential elections. At 11:15 p.m. EST on Election Day, major broadcast stations called the swing state of Ohio for Obama. An hour later, Romney gave a gracious concession speech, followed by Obama's call for unity. A country of 317 million accepted the results just an hour after the polls closed in the Pacific Time Zone, with Hawaii and Alaska still open. It was simply amazing to watch! How could we do this in the Philippines, a country more densely populated than any state in America? It is the size of Arizona but ten times its population; one-third the population of America, but with only three percent of its area. It is also very young (68 years, if reckoned from US-granted independence, or 115, if from the defeat of the Spanish). Understandably, most of the government processes are still in flux.

But there is more to America than just a working electoral process. I love her public service institutions. They say that there are more libraries in America than there are McDonald's stores! Each county issued library cards to us even if we would only be in the area for a few weeks. Community and senior centers allowed use of their facilities, often without charge. As RVers, we also have a deep appreciation for the world's largest road network, almost four million miles, seamlessly interconnected from coast to coast. Someday, however, we wish there could be national fishing licenses for Americans on the move like us. The National Parks Service has no equal in the world! Through Bill's Senior Golden Pass, we have camped in four and visited, for free, thirty-three of the forty-nine National Parks, eighty-two National Monuments and Historical Sites and both national parkways. I now have my Pass, also for just $10 lifetime, obtained from one of the parks. Canadian and British equivalents are expensive with high annual fees.

Then there is that which you cannot find elsewhere in the world: the unequaled diversity of the American people whose dreams are unimaginable and achievements unprecedented. In our travels, we have met many everyday heroes and brave pioneers who came to this country and fulfilled their dreams. We have been to thirty of the forty-four American Presidents' homes, tombs, and presidential libraries. And I have been moved by literary greats who have preserved this compelling American story. We saw, heard, touched, tasted, and smelled America.

Admittedly, there are huge criticisms of this world power: individualism, capitalism, and imperialism, to name a few. I have always believed in the exercise of free will, in the hard work of the individual and, so for me, capitalism is not evil, greed is! As noted in Dinesh d'Souza's controversial documentary, America does not amass "wealth by conquest;" it builds "wealth by innovation." And I, however old, am proud to be part of the fresh blood that fuels innovation.

True, in the past four years my dancing had changed from disco and ballroom to country and rock. My fashion sense, if there ever was any, had shifted from blouses and skirts to tank tops and jeans (or shorts). Grilled burgers, steaks, and pies have gradually inched out *adobo*, *pancit*, and *lumpia* from my kitchen. But these do not mean I am no longer a Filipino! I still readily shift to Tagalog when I am with my countrymen, and I still think in Tagalog most of the time. That's why I confuse genders, often conspicuously because there is hardly such a thing in Tagalog. The word for son or daughter is the same: *anak*; wife or husband: *asawa*; brother or sister: *kapatid*. Although some connote gender, like *kuya* for an elder brother, *ate* an elder sister. And it would be difficult for me to consider a sandwich a meal, it doesn't have rice!

I still feel proud when I learn about Filipino accomplishments, like when the island of Palawan bested the islands of the world, or when Vigan became one of the seven new wonder cities. When Megan Young was crowned Miss World, the Philippines became the only country that has won all five of the major beauty titles. By association, people might consider me attractive, too! Since Jessica Sanchez almost became American Idol, I have become more confident in karaoke sessions. I even felt triumphant when Floyd Mayweather agreed to take on our Manny Pacquiao!

Throughout our cruising, I became keenly aware of the kinship between the Philippines and America. They share the blue waters of the Pacific Ocean and the treacherous Pacific Ring of Fire. The Spanish colonized the American Southwest and the Philippines for almost the same number of years. The United States laid the foundation for a modern Philippines for fifty years after the 300-year Spanish rule. Filipinos fought side by side with Americans in WWII. And now, countless Filipino nurses, teachers, and seamen are an integral part of US hospitals, schools, and ships. July 4 is not just America's Independence Day for me. On that day in 1946, the United States gave us our own independence, 170 years after she got hers. It had been declared Filipino-American Friendship Day in the Philippines.

There are also many differences. The Philippines is a tropical archipelago of 7,107 islands; the United States, except for Hawaii and Alaska, a vast contiguous temperate land. Plants and wildlife are different. I have to pay top dollar in Asian stores for many much-missed tropical fruits. The wide vistas of the Great Plains, the expansive desert of the Southwest, and the giant glaciers of Alaska are worlds apart from what I've seen in my native land. As I toured America, I often felt sad for the Philippines. Who wouldn't when you see that here parents of students in elementary and high schools see the progress of their kids online? But then I remember, the Philippines is only 68 years old; the United States, already 238. There is a lot of time to grow!

I am so lucky to have both: the experience of a developed world and the dreams of a developing country. That is why I wanted, nay, needed to be a dual citizen. I did not cease to be a Filipino. My natural citizenship was only taken away! On October 3, 2013, I took another oath at the Philippine Consulate in LA and re-pledged my loyalty to the Philippines. I became a Filipino-American. I did not get boiled into the thick soup melting in the pot. Instead, I got included in a colorful, chunky stew—contributing to the taste, but retaining enough of my unique flavor.

Changing Carolina Forever

On October 16, 2013 we arrived at the Viewpoint RV Golf and Tennis Resort for a meaningful pause. It would be a break from being constantly on the move. And it would be winter in sunny, warm, and dry weather. The spacious campsite even had a young tree at a corner that gave us fresh oranges every day. Friendly neighbors on Lane 5500 welcomed us to the Resort.

We had made four cross-continent runs in a little over four years. Travel does drive deep change! I became a US citizen in the Northwest. In the Northeast, I was moved, converted and became an American. Back in Seattle I realized I had become a wife. Finally, in LA I returned to my roots and became a Filipino-American. I had become forever changed.

We no longer wish to travel full time. We have not yet decided to nest as in Option 5 when we will buy another sticks and bricks house that, hopefully, will be our last. In the meantime, we will cover the world from an Arizona base. During late spring, summer, and early fall when Arizona sizzles, we will go somewhere outside of America or visit family. And, when that time of year comes, we can be as excited as we were in the beginning when we started to cruise. There will be time for rest between trips.

After our first winter in Viewpoint, we traveled to nine countries in Europe from May to August of 2014. We flew to Norway, Sweden, and Finland and cruised to Russia, Iceland, and the United Kingdom, including Scotland and Ireland. Then we went on a road trip through England, and Wales—building the tour around April's wedding in Scotland. After a second winter in Viewpoint, we have come back from Dubai, Italy, Spain, France, and London. We will also go to Hawaii to complete the United States and end the year with visits to six other countries.

A family doctor has traced my health issues to undiagnosed and untreated hypothyroidism and nascent hypertension. A maintenance regimen of half of the smallest doses of the thyroid hormone and a diuretic is in place. My sleep is now restful, and I am no longer using those sleep-inducing mood-altering pills other doctors on the road had prescribed for me. Although GERD is still there (I still eat too fast and talk too much), hives have not reappeared for a year.

We have also found our spiritual home in Holy Cross Catholic Church where Bill is an active member of the Knights of Columbus chapter. He regularly plays tennis, while I try to catch up, now that I have a complete tennis wardrobe! I frequent the fitness center, sing at karaoke sessions and try to play Texas Hold'Em whenever I can. We both party with friends and neighbors and find many good events to go to in the Phoenix area, like Super Bowl XLIX!

Bill also plays golf but finds the best fulfillment in being a Court-appointed Special Advocate (CASA) of a sixteen-year-old boy. While he is out with him or attending meetings, I plan and cook healthy, easy, and yummy vegetable dishes with as little meat as possible. And, of course, I get glued to my laptop, imagining things, weaving words, and exercising, with my fingers.

When Bill and I married, I had already cooked and taught a little. Bill took me traveling and taught me how to love. During our travels, I met people who egged me to write. Literary greats inspired me no end. Now that I have completed this book, even if I don't sell many copies, Bill and I will enjoy rereading the book a third time or more, rocking in our chairs. In short, all of my five goals have been achieved. My life philosophy of dreaming and daring has again proved right! As Marcel Proust said, "The real voyage of discovery consists not in seeking new landscapes, but in having new eyes." I have new eyes, and not just from the cataract surgery. They are Filipino-American eyes. My new calling card says it best. Carolina Esguerra Colborn. Wanderer. Writer. Wife.

APPENDICES

Appendix 1:
Different Kinds of RVs

There are two general classifications of recreational vehicles (RVs): motorized and non-motorized. The motorized version includes the living area as well as the engine and drivetrain in one vehicular unit. The second is a complete housing unit that is pulled or towed by a motor vehicle powerful enough to do just that.

Motorhomes

There are four kinds of motorized RVs according to sizes, from the smallest camper van to the biggest Class As. Camper vans are vans retrofitted to create a small, walkable area at the back. These are very popular in Europe where the roads are pretty narrow. Bigger than camper vans are Class Cs that can go up to almost thirty feet in length. The distinctive feature of a Class C is a sleeping area on top of the driver's compartment. Typically, a Class C is complete with a kitchen, a dinette, and a bathroom. Class B motorhomes are similar in size but have the sleeping area at the back. Class As are usually upwards of thirty feet in length. They can also be fitted with slide-outs (as many as five) that make the living areas much bigger when parked. These Class As (sometimes, some of the larger Class Bs and Cs, too) can tow a dinghy, a dolly for cars or even a big toy hauler.

Tag-along or Trailer   **Fifth Wheel**

Non-motorized RVs

There are two kinds of non-motorized RVs: travel trailers or fifth-wheels. Travel trailers are towable housing units of various sizes, from the lighter pop-ups to teardrop campers, to the bigger Airstreams and even more major ones. They are towed by vehicles that have enough power for their size. On the other hand, fifth wheels are usually larger and feature big noses that house the bedrooms. Those noses fit over and attach to beds of powerful pick-up trucks, making the attachment more secure and stable. They are usually as big as Class As and, like the larger travel trailers, can use slide-outs to expand living areas.

Appendix 2:
Five Options in RV Cruising

Option 1: Escaping

Escaping is the option when you still need to do things in one place and just want to pause to be recharged in another. You may be a student, an employee, an executive, a business owner, or a housewife with a nagging urge to escape from everyday life. You want the benefits of cruising, without suffering the disadvantages of being away from a base. Weekends are RV getaways.

Option 2: Sightseeing

When you finally have more time to attend to the bucket list that had grown long because you could not escape often enough, you may use an RV for a longer vacation. Stay for three or four days per stop; there is no need to pack or unpack. Go to your next stop and spend three or four days there. Keep on going this way until you have covered as much distance as you would like to chip away at that bucket list and that your vacation time allows you to do.

Option 3: Sightseeing *cum* Relaxing

With a larger living space, you can select a base for lounging around and entertaining friends. Then you can explore the areas around your base by sight-seeing using your dinghy for day trips or even trips of a couple or a few days. Once you think you have rested enough or have seen what you wanted to cover in an area, you can then drive to another base and repeat the process.

Option 4: Snow-birding

Snow-birding is to be in a general area for the season, much like birds do. It means that, during the summer months, one stays in the cooler north (in America or outside the country). In the winter months, it means being in the warmer south (in America or outside the country). It also means roaming less and finding more activities to do where you snow-bird.

Option 5: Nesting

Nesting comes when you may no longer have much energy for travel. A nest is selected and established, your locale for most of the year. Travels will be limited to visits with family during major holidays or birthdays or to favorite spots for escaping. Thus, it would have to be at a location central to children's residences or one they would like to visit.

Appendix 3:
Economics of the RV Cruising Lifestyle

	LIVING AT HOME	PREVIOUS RVing	CONTEMPLATED RVing
FUEL EXPENSES	350	2000	500
VEHICLE MAINTENANCE	150	300	500
CAMPSITE FEES/UTILITIES	850	550	350
FOOD AND HOUSEHOLD SUPPLIES	400	400	400
RECREATION AND ENTERTAINMENT	500	100	100
HEALTH MAINTENANCE	750	750	750
INSURANCE AND TAXES	500	100	150
TOTAL	3500	4150	2650

Fuel Expenses

In the previous option, Option 2, fuel costs ran from about $1,500 to over $2,000 per month. It was the time of going to different places and staying only three to four nights, covering a lot of miles. We used a scooter for going around nearby towns. In the option we were contemplating, Option 3, fuel cost would be substantially less than the previous one, even if the rig is bigger because we would stay longer at a place.

Vehicle Ownership and Maintenance

Unlike houses, RVs do not appreciate in value. They are homes on wheels that are regularly subjected to the rigors of the road. Buying a brand-new one, therefore, does not make sense. Like cars, their values take a deep dive in the first year or two; we would rather let other people take that hit. Investment in properties is no longer high on our agenda.

All in all, the monthly cost of ownership (depreciation + maintenance) for a home on wheels is around $500 per month, should a new rig last ten years, and double if only five. Not bad for a space of about 350 square feet, translating to less than $1.50 per month per square feet, just slightly above the cost of rented living space in Kent, Washington. However, the condos will be there long after we pass on while the rig will most probably become unusable even before we do.

Campsite Fees/Utilities

In the previous Option, a Camp Club USA membership and a Senior Golden Pass gave 50 percent off for camping fees, which ranged anywhere from $10 to $70 a night. We averaged $350–$450 a month. In Option 3, the upgraded TT membership would result in camping expenses of a little over $3 a day or $100 per month if we use it full-time for the next thirteen years. If we only use it for half the time or full-time in 6.5 years, it will double to $200. To equal previous expenses for campsites, the network just has to be used for a third of the time or 4.3 years, full-time.

Furthermore, exterior maintenance of a home (like landscaping) can be significantly more expensive than those for an RV. Parks and resorts take care of this. There may also be association dues that can be as high as $350 a month for condos. TT fees include even power, water, and sewer; sometimes even cable and Wi-Fi. Thus, expenses for utilities are almost eliminated (except for cell phone costs).

Taxes and Insurance

An RV is a second home, or if you are full-timing, it is the primary. Sales/excise tax on the purchase of the RV and interest on future payments are just like those on a traditional home or second home. However, since an RV is not real property, property tax is nil. Insurance on the trailer/fifth wheel is lower than on home insurance; but, since a motor home is a motorized vehicle, insurance is higher.

Recreation and Entertainment

Entertainment and recreational expenses are not big because cruising takes you not only to new places but also visits to family and friends. While living in a home, expenses for family outings and other out-of-town visits would be much more. Costs would include fuel for the car (or fare for other types of transportation used), motel fees, and other charges associated with going to another place.

Appendix 4:
Resources around Campgrounds

There are available resources for fun other than the amenities and activities in a campground or the tourist spots in the nearby area. We have been amazed at the possibilities.

Public Centers

There are public centers, like libraries, which offer a steady supply of DVDs, CDs, magazines, and books. Visitor Centers are sources of info and discount coupons, great for outlying areas like the Yukon. Community centers are suitable substitutes for gyms when the campground does not have a fitness center. Senior centers are also a resource once you admit you are already a senior!

Educational institutions

Colleges and universities are also heaven-sent. At Gonzaga University in Spokane, Washington, for example, we found the Bing Crosby House. At Western Washington University in Bellingham, Washington, there are 33 sculptures of renowned artists all around the campus. Plays, concerts, symphonies, etc., also abound in educational institutions.

Religious Institutions

Then there are religious institutions. Churches have other functions aside from Sunday services. Cultural events, spiritual retreats, lectures, and seminars, and choir concerts are always available.

Commercial Establishments

Countless commercial establishments compete for our dollars. Even thrift stores such as the Goodwill Chain of Stores, St. Vincent de

Paul, Salvation Army, or the Habitat for Humanity's ReStore are treasure-hunting grounds. Those near affluent communities are best. Factory outlet malls are great for the budget and serve as treadmill substitutes. Second-run movie houses are places for much cheaper ($2.50) movies.

GO (Government Organizations) or NGO (Non-government Organizations) Events

City, county or state governments or civic and other associations often sponsor events for the benefit of communities, like Farmers' Markets, Art Crawls, Village Dances, etc.

Homes of Family and Friends

Your family's or friends' homes are resources you can always count on. Their driveways can be places to park an RV, and they may even connect you to power and water.

Appendix 5:
Criteria for Choosing an RV

	QUALITY SCORE	FINANCIAL SCORE	NOTES
BASIC REQUIREMENTS	50%		mpg, age, miles traveled, living space, slides
OUR NEEDS	30%		enclosed toilet, office desk, sleeper sofa
OUR WANTS	20%		washer/dryer, large TV
OVERALL QUALITY SCORE			
ONE-TIME EXPENSES		50%	down payment or cash payment
RECURRING EXPENSES		40%	monthly amortization, repairs, insurance
SALVAGE VALUES		10%	resale value
OVERALL FINANCIAL SCORE			
OVERALL SCORE	60%	40%	

We obtained Quality Score by assigning weights to three factors. Basic requirements include the efficiency of the vehicle in mpg, if motorized, age of the vehicle, miles traveled, living and storage space available, including number of slides. Needs include features that you absolutely must have, and Wants are pluses that you would rather also have. You may vary the weights assigned depending on your situation or preferences.

You can derive the Financial Score by giving weights to one-time and recurring expenses and salvage value. If the RV will be purchased through a loan, the down payment (if paid in cash, then the whole amount) is the one-time part, and the monthly amortization is the recurring one. Recurring costs also include foreseeable repairs and maintenance in both scenarios. Salvage or resale value is the amount at which you think the market will buy the unit after you have used it for the time intended. You can change the weights as you deem fit.

We used the Quality and Financial Scores to get the Overall Score, giving them appropriate weights: 60% for quality and 40% for financial. You may revise the weights, based on what is more important to you at the time of purchase.

Appendix 6:
Four Kinds of Campgrounds

A campsite is usually anywhere from 15 to 25 feet wide and from 40 to 80 feet long for our RV size, with space for a tow vehicle. Campgrounds are of four different kinds. Assuming Location is the y-axis, and Amenities/Activities as the x-axis, then you have four quadrants. As you go higher on the y-axis, it is from urban to rural. On the x-axis, on the other hand, as you move from left to right, it is from no amenities or activities to a ton of them.

```
                    y-axis  | more amenities
                            |
                            |
          Quadrant 1        |     Quadra nt 2
          NATURE RV RESORT  |     CITY RV RESORT
                            |
  away ─────────────────────┼──────────────────── x-axis
  from city                 |               nearer city
                            |
          Quadrant 3        |     Quadrant 4
          NATURE PARK       |     CITY PARK
                            |
                            | less amenities
```

A **Nature RV Resort** is in Quadrant 1; that is, campgrounds that are in more rural places and have more amenities/activities. The Green Mountain RV Resort at the outskirts of Lenoir, North Carolina, near the Blue Ridge Parkway, is like this. Sites have a sizable deck, looking out to a fresh spring, which you can use for private socials. It is very hilly with lots of large trees. Aside from a clubhouse with billiards, table tennis and other game tables, it has a nine-hole golf course, tennis and volleyball courts and a lake for fishing and boating. Live bands play at Saturday dances.

A **City RV Resort** is in Quadrant 2, located at or near a city and with more amenities/activities. TT Orlando in Orlando, Florida is an example. It is just six miles away from the Disney World and within walking distance of strip malls and big grocery and other chains. It has a large clubhouse with games, billiards, table tennis, large TV room, a gift shop, and a restaurant. Outside there are an exercise room, hot tubs, pools, tennis courts, horseshoe pits, volleyball courts, and mini-golf course. There may also be many activities and clubs to join.

A **City RV Park** is in Quadrant 3, found at or near a city but with minimal amenities/activities. It is used primarily to be near a family or friends with whom we would like to visit or a base from which to explore a city's attractions. The French Quarter RV Resort near the French Quarter of New Orleans is an example.

A **Nature RV Park** is in Quadrant 4, that is, in a more rural area but with minimal amenities/activities, what you need when you want to get away from it all. State and national parks, as well as parts of our national forests, Corps of Engineers' land preserves, beach enclaves, etc., are mostly like this. The best one that comes to mind is the National Forest Service campground along Big Sur, overlooking the Pacific Ocean. Some national parks, such as Joshua Tree National Park, qualify; bigger national parks with lots of facilities, such as Yosemite and Yellowstone, do not.

NOTE: Nature RV Resorts and Nature RV Parks are best for Options 1 and 3. A City RV Park is always an option for Option 5. Option 2 can be in any of the campgrounds. A City RV Resort would be perfect for Option 4 or extended stays.

Appendix 7:
Utilizing Technology on the Go

Technology is the total of state-of-the-art means (specific methods, materials, and devices) used to solve practical problems. Today's means include hardware, software, practices, materials, etc. Practical problems of cruising in an RV include staying in contact with distant family and friends and minimizing weight on the RV to reduce fuel expenses. Getting to new destinations through unfamiliar roads and documenting the enjoyment of new places, activities, and friends are others. Being prepared for all kinds of conditions (no power, getting stranded, etc.), and being able to find whatever we need are also two of the more practical problems.

General Purpose Gadgets

We use a laptop, a tablet, and sometimes even a smartphone for electronically keeping and updating files, banking, paying bills, writing posts, and processing other documents. We also use them for e-mailing and chatting, especially with video, with family and friends anywhere they are around the world. The Kindle also now holds for us about a hundred odd books. Smartphones are very handy when we find ourselves in dire situations away from home.

GPSs now have extra wide screens, give real-time traffic alerts and other information, and even cater specifically to RVers' needs. Together with smartphones, they always provide a guide to where you need to go. It can be the next campground, the nearest Costco, or where you can find a Redbox kiosk. You may also be looking for a type of food to eat, the local attraction you do not want to miss, the nearest gas station, or the closest public dump/fresh water station. These are all necessities of being in and around new places most of the time.

The DSLR camera has been great for taking superb shots of outstanding scenery and events. We have two types of lenses to take care of different situations, action shots, and other changing requirements. The DSLR gives greater control than a point-and-click camera does and allows for higher resolutions for better quality pictures. However, it is bulkier. Nowadays, cell phone or iPad cameras provide many more advanced features.

RV Technology

Homes on wheels also require lots of technologies. Systems are mostly satellite-based so that things are operable wherever you may end up. There are also different kinds of systems available for all types of situations, and the devices are usually more compact and made of lighter material than those in regular homes.

Let us take power, for instance. On the road or while dry camping, the refrigerator runs on LPG. Parked at a full-hookup campground, it draws power, like all other appliances and lights, from a 30 or 50-amp circuit. We prefer 50 because of the load we have; using many devices at the same time usually breaks the 30-amp circuit. When you dry camp, lights are run by house batteries while the generator runs all others such as air conditioning, oven, etc.

Plumbing is also different with three different tank systems. You can hook up to city water or store water in the fresh water tank. The "gray water" tank holds the water from the sinks, shower and washing machine/dryer combo. The "black water" tank holds–you guessed it–the water from the toilet. You have to make sure they are all regularly drained and flushed. You also have to use RV-friendly toilet paper that dissolves more quickly in water.

Most campgrounds have hookups to sewer dumps on the campsite itself to take care of this. But when they don't, or when you are parked at Walmart or a rest area, public or for-pay dump stations may be necessary between stays. Other times you may use portable holding tanks called blue boys or honey wagons. Sometimes, the campground may also allow a service provider that comes out to the park to drain tanks of RVs camped there.

Appendix 8:
My Different Notions of Fun*

	ALONE	WITH SOMEONE
FREE-SPIRITED	writing in a journal taking photos reading a book	tubing, canoeing, kayaking hiking a trail snorkeling
STRUCTURED	attending a talk hearing mass painting	playing bridge, poker or mahjong dancing a choreography working out in a gym
ORDINARY	making a shopping list doing puzzles watching TV	sitting around a campfire dining potluck going to the theater
UNORDINARY	planning a trip finding a bargain hosting a party	going to a concert watching a play organizing a group presentation
LIGHTHEARTED	riding a carousel surfing on the net playing online games	singing at a karaoke session dancing at a party playing board games
FIRST TIME	flying a kite riding a bike skating	riding a hot air balloon riding a roller coaster riding a helicopter
REPETITIVE	watering plants cooking meals decorating the house	visiting with friends eating out taking a road trip

* Above are **my** different notions of fun. Your examples may be different. Fun can either be done alone or with someone. There can also be different kinds: free-spirited versus structured, ordinary versus unordinary, lighthearted, first-time versus repetitive. You can build your own matrix of fun things to do, so you don't forget a single one, and you have a range of options when boredom suddenly strikes.

Appendix 9:
10 Commandments of Full-time RV Cruising

1. Choose an RV that meets basic needs.

The RV must be small yet meet basic needs because miles per gallon (mpg) rules. With the price of gas or diesel, you have to balance the space required and the money spent for fuel. The same thing goes for the dinghy. We did not opt for a fifth wheel because we ran around a lot, and they are towed by a pick-up truck, which usually has low mpg.

2. Always travel light.

Travel light was also our motto when we had to take business trips. In the RV lifestyle, this is the golden rule. Remember that you are always moving your home, so live with the barest minimum. A very useful tip is: do not buy anything new without throwing any old thing out in exchange. Or, buy only what is consumable in a week; do not stock pile!

3. Become a member of a network.

TT is a network of eighty campgrounds in North America. There will be no need to camp in other parks except for rare instances or when you want to stay at a particular resort or a famous national park. You will find that you can reduce camping expenses and the chore of looking for campgrounds is eliminated.

4. Use the best mail-forwarding service.

You may want to take advantage of lower tax rates and use mailing addresses from post office boxes in states such as South and North Dakota, Montana, Texas, Arizona, Florida, etc. The mail-forwarding companies provide all sorts of services.We use a family member's home address because we were told that mailed-in voting is limited to those with actual home addresses.

5. Use nationwide services or buy locally, whichever makes better sense.

When you have something to do or buy for your RV or dinghy or any appliance, it is best to use nationwide chains that honor the quality of their service or product anywhere. As we had experienced, Camping World is the best service provider for our RV needs. It is not contradictory to buying locally. For higher-value products and services, it is best to go with nationwide chains, but for simpler jobs and lower-value goods, it is an excellent practice to contribute to the local economy. Besides, flea and farmers' markets sell the season's best produce and the community's best crafts at the lowest prices.

6. Stay healthy, and build healthcare needs into your plan.

This commandment was not part of our original ten. We found ourselves driven more by schedules of family, friends or circumstances. If we had to redo some things, we would make sure we had three months a year with a consistent family doctor (centrally located within your travels).

7. Look for work or payback opportunities that blend with the lifestyle.

You don't have to give up earning income or practicing some ministry to enjoy cruising. Many of those we meet in the road work with seasonal job opportunities in different parts of the country. Workamping.com lists a host of job opportunities. Habitat for Humanity welcomes RVers in its Care-a-Vanners program; so do Amazon's fulfillment centers across the country. Sometimes, they even provide the campsites. I have dreamed of turning our RV to a SOW, Soup-on-Wheels, and taking them to church grounds to feed the hungry.

8. Stay connected to friends and family.

Don't be afraid; use technology! The hardest part of this life is having to be far from your loved ones. Technology bridges the gap. Facebook has been most useful, especially now with the free call feature. Skype with the video feature is awesome. Hangouts even gave me calls with three or more people around the world. There are numerous other apps that make the connection easy and alive.

9. Plan and document your trips well.

Enjoying the places and activities is only one-third of the fun. Another third is planning and visualizing the fun. The last third is reliving the fun. Thus, you should document as best as you can. Again, technology is a must. A DSLR and a camera phone have been indispensable to us. Blogging is simply digital journaling, and Pinterest is just a digital scrapbook.

10. Follow the sun to maximize the fun.

For maximum enjoyment, don't forget that you do not need to shiver in the cold nor blister in the sun. Commandment Ten is the most important, the main reason for cruising in an RV. Spend summers in the north and winters nearer the equator.

If you are full-timing in an RV, there is an additional commandment: Don't trade your home for a motorized vehicle. True, you are gung-ho about this cruising lifestyle; but what if something happens and you have to go back to staying put? You may no longer have the funds to buy a new home. Choose an RV that you can pay for in cash, so you do not have to sell a home or incur new debt. If you can, rent out your house. If you have qualms about your home deteriorating, then full-time RVing may not be for you. You might as well live in your home part of the time.

Extended List of Acknowledgments

They say that "The only ones who truly know your story are the ones who help you write them." The following people made our travels memorable, but I could not include all their names within the narrative. They visited with us; we visited with them, and we met each other at campgrounds or other places for meetings or reunions. I have tried to identify all of them in this Extended List of Acknowledgments. Hopefully, I did not forget anyone. If I did, please forgive me!

1. My children and their families
   a. Trisha, husband Deejay, and children Krishna, Daniela, and Kenji
   b. Claudine, husband Arnold, and children Enzo, Kai, and Anfernee and stepchildren Ashton and Andre
   c. April, husband Clint, and their baby on the way
2. Bill's children and their families
   a. Jim, wife Ana, and children Madeline and Ben
   b. Suzanne, husband Dean, and children Devin and Cassie
   c. Cristine, husband Mitch, and son Kyle
3. My sisters and some of their family members
   a. Cynthia, husband Roger, and daughter Christine
   b. Julie, daughter Erika and husband Jesse
   c. Cherry, husband Rick, and daughter Zan and her husband Harley
4. My other relatives in America
   a. From San Diego: Tia Juana (now deceased) and son Polly; Ate Tesing and Kuya Ute and their children and families
   b. From Chicago (and Rosario, Batangas): Ate Piling, Tony and Nora, and other children and their families; Ate Ofreng; Ate Belen and her friend Araceli; and Ate Amor
4. Bill's sister, Rosemary, husband Jack and her family
   a. Joe and wife Susan
   b. Bill and partner Kevin
   c. Becky and husband Tommy
5. My friends from the Philippines
   a. I/ACT: Ann; Dittas; Fides and husband Benjie; Loy, wife Lilet, and his children; Lea, husband Jimmy, and their children; Peng; Watet; Glenda and Ariel; Tess

b. IBM: Tony and wife Bernie

c. Toastmasters: Angie and husband Wendell

d. DAP: May, Jingjing and her friends John and his wife Marilou: Cynthia and her friends

6. Our friends from Seattle, Washington

a. Susie and Don

b. Book Club: Sheila and Bill; Liz and Michael (now deceased); Clyde; Merry and Dave; Sandy and Jerry

c. Estrogen Club: Inja and husband; Kathleen and husband; Cathy and husband; Yim; Stephanie; and Pam

d. from a West Seattle parish: Fr. Jack; John and wife Marsha

e. St. John the Baptist Parish: Irene and Fred; Tita and husband

7. Bill's friends

a. Pittsburg High School: Jack and wife Joy; Jim and wife Carol; Doug and wife Audrey; Sam and wife Kathy; Gretchen and husband Don; Roxanne and husband John.

b. Members of the Organizing Committee for the PHS 50th Reunion: Sandy, Carolyn, Charlie and Terry, Gary and Jo, Ron and Sharon, and Vicky and Ken. And other classmates we met at the Reunion of the PHS class of '62.

c. Sigma Chi of Pittsburg State University: Oliver and wife Kris; Jim and wife Glenda; and other Sigma Chi brothers and their spouses

d. Former workmates Terry, Gene, and Glen and wife Debbie (now deceased)

8. Friends we met while cruising

a. Joe and Dottie

b. Silly Willy and Fluffy

c. Bev and Dan

d. Thelma and Tom (now deceased), Dolores and Randy

e. Roberta and Tim

f. Suzy and Fred (now deceased)

g. Jane and Mike

h. Paul

i. Jure and Katarina from Slovenia

j. Sizzy and Jeanne

k. Friends from Viewpoint: Bud and Bonnie; Mel and Carolyn; Chris and Bonnie; Ken and Sharon; Wayne and Val; Cam and Clinkie; members of the Viewpoint Tennis Club; and many others

About the Author

Carolina Esguerra Colborn was prominent in Philippine business before she migrated to the US in 2004. She was former President/CEO of BayanTrade, the e-procurement hub of the Philippines, and Managing Director of SAP Philippines. She also served as Deputy Commissioner of the Bureau of Internal Revenue, General Manager of MegaLink, the ATM switch of banks, and Vice-President of the Development Academy of the Philippines. Before serving in these positions, she also worked for Andersen Consulting (now Accenture), IBM and NCR. She holds a BS in Mathematics, MBA, and DPA abd from the University of the Philippines.

In industry, she was President of the Philippine Computer Society, founding Chair of the Information Technology Foundation of the Philippines, and founding President of the Knowledge Management Association of the Philippines. In the Southeast Asia Computer Confederation, she was Chair of the Special Industry Group on Professional Standards and SEARCC Expo 1990, a biennial regional computer convention. Twice a recipient of the Most Powerful Women in IT Award, she represented the private sector in the National Information Technology Council.

Carolina settled in Seattle, Washington where her eldest daughter lives. While babysitting her grandson, she taught at the Seattle Central Community College, Central Washington University, and Renton Technical College. She also volunteered for SCORE, the Service Corps of Retired Executives. In 2007, she met Bill Colborn on the Net. Soon after their wedding in 2008, Bill sold his business, and they started their cruise of North America in an RV. She maintains a blog on their journeys, five posts of which have been published elsewhere. They now travel the world from a base in Phoenix, Arizona.

Website: http://www.carolcolborn.wix.com/carolinacruising
Blog: http://rvcruisinglifestyle.blogspot.com
Email: carol.colborn@gmail.com

Social Media Handles:
Facebook Fan Page: Carol Esguerra Colborn (also Carol Carreon)
Facebook Business Page: Carolina: Cruising
Twitter: carolcruisng
Instagram: carolcolborn
Pinterest: Carolina Colborn